Race: Migration and Integration

RACE

Migration and Integration

by

JEREMIAH NEWMAN

Professor of Sociology

Maynooth

HELICON
Baltimore

Helicon Press, Inc.
1120 N. Calvert Street
Baltimore, Maryland 21202

Library of Congress Catalog Card Number 67-14645

PRINTED AND BOUND IN THE REPUBLIC OF IRELAND
BY CAHILL AND COMPANY LIMITED, DUBLIN

Contents

3

5

Race: Migration and Integration

Introduction

Despite the flood of books and articles on various aspects of the race question, which have been appearing in recent years, there has been no effort at any comprehensive treatment of the matter from both a global and Christian point of view.

The present work aims at supplying this want. It is particularly concerned with the interconnection of the questions of race and migration and endeavors to study them in relationship one to the other.

Its special interest is with ethical precepts and Christian perspectives, which one can readily accept as a member of any of the Christian Churches. It is for this reason that it relegates its analysis of official Church pronouncements to appendices. The principles contained therein run right through the preceding chapters.

However, since the book was first undertaken there have been many developments and it has been by no means easy to keep pace with them. It is therefore with apologies to the reader for its inevitable brevity that I summarize here, in the shadow of the assassination of Dr. Martin Luther King in America, and the controversy following Mr. Enoch Powell's speech relative to the impending Race Relations Act in Great Britain, the immediate background against which this book must be read.

In Britain events during the years 1967 and 1968 to date have underlined both the growing dimensions of the problems of race relations and colored immigration for Britain and the utter inadequacy of existing legislative measures for dealing with them.

It has taken a long time to convince the British public in general—and the British government in particular—of the stern truth of this. When, in December, 1966, private members' bills were introduced in both the Commons and the Lords to extend the 1965 Race Relations Act to housing, employment and credit facilities, there was considerable skepticism about the need for this. One heard the view expressed, for example, that—in much the same way as had to be done during the nineteenth century in order to ensure proper working conditions in factories—what was needed was not so much a new law as a new form of law enforcement.[1]

There were some experienced students of the question to be found who were even disposed to contend that racial prejudice and discrimination was something more apparent than real in Britain. Thus Mr. R. B. Davison, in his book *Black British*, wrote: "Racial frictions in British industry are minimal, and such tensions as do arise occur in no greater or lesser degree than they would among heterogeneous groups of workers anywhere".[2] Similarly, Miss Sheila Patterson, writing in an issue of *New Society* devoted especially to the color problem, maintained that, while there was indeed some discrimination in the field of employment and the like, there was very little that could be labeled simply "racial". In most cases attitudes were conditioned by complex factors, including such as suspicion of an untried labor force, and language and cultural difficulties.[3] She claimed that the kind of evidence of discrimination assembled by bodies like CARD and the Society of Labor Lawyers tends to focus on the experiences of a vocal minority of immigrants, the ones who—for whatsoever reason—feel ill-treated.

The publication, in April, 1967, of a thorough survey—commissioned by the Race Relations Board and carried out by PEP—brought new facts to light and ended the argument. Taking the three disputed areas which had been omitted from the 1965 Race Relations Act—housing, employment and the provision of insurance and credit facilities—and submitting the evidence alleged by immigrants to rigorous tests—this survey showed conclusively that there was indeed a good deal of racial discrimination in Britain, despite the existence of legislative machinery designed to avoid it. Writing in the *New Statesman*, Mr. Dipak Nandy of the University of Kent summarized it well: "We know the facts now. When colored immigrants apply for jobs they can expect to be turned away on grounds of color or race on at least two occasions out of every five, and probably much more frequently; when they apply for private lodgings they can expect refusal on two occasions out of three; when they try to buy a house they can expect discrimination on two occasions out of three; when they try to insure their cars they can expect outright refusals or higher premiums on four occasions out of five; and when they try to hire a car, they can expect either higher deposits or higher charges on two occasions out of every three."[4]

The fact that Mr. Nandy is a member of CARD's executive did not weaken his argument; it simply could not do so. *The Sunday Times* came out with a vigorous editorial (23 April, 1967), which declared that the survey had provided "proof positive" of discrimination in the domains in question, and that it had "exploded the gradualist myth" by making the need for further legislation crystal clear. It called for immediate steps to remedy the situation: "Just as in the government, with a few honorable exceptions, there is a discreditable want of leadership, so in the cities there is a complacent belief that sleeping dogs will lie. As a policy for race relations this is a disastrous illusion."

The Observer—typically liberal—would go even further: "We are embarked on the irreversible course of being a multi-racial society. At present, the immigrant community is about one million strong. By the end of the century, on present trends, it may be about three times that number. And, unless we are prepared to take far-reaching action now, it will then be a community of three million second-class citizens" (Editorial, 23 April, 1967).

But are the British people quite ready for the full implications of a multi-racial society? Its creation is not simply the elimination of discrimination of the kind referred to but full integration and —ultimately—miscegenation. The average Englishman balks easily at this prospect. It must not be forgotten that by the end of 1967 there were only six colored policemen (all recently appointed) and ten colored magistrates. There were no colored members of Parliament and no black men on the town councils of cities with large colored populations.

On the other hand there is a growing chorus of colored voices that all these things are due as rights.[5] Black leaders are promising to achieve their attainment and formerly mild movements, like CARD and the West Indian Standing Conference, are becoming more militant. Michael X is the living symbol of their attitude: "I was taught in school that England was the mother country. White Englishman, don't tell *me* to go home. I *am* home."[6]

Since the 1964 visit of Malcolm X and that of Stokely Carmichael in 1967, this militancy has grown quite rapidly. So much so in fact that the government found it advisable to ban the return of the latter in an effort to stem the developing consciousness on the part of its colored immigrant minority that, like the American Negroes, it too could fashion a kind of "Black Power". And does not Michael X, the practicing Muslim, and his Racial Adjustment Action Society, resemble a British version of the American Black Muslim movement? Britain today is becoming ever more painfully aware of the "Black Man in Search of Power".[7]

For these reasons the man in the street might well be pardoned for being a little fearful of measures designed to further the emergence of a multi-racial society. And in point of fact in May, 1967, a *Sunday Times* poll, conducted by the Opinion

Research Center, showed that, while a small majority of people in Britain would be prepared to favor the extension of the powers of the Race Relations Board to cover jobs and housing, there was also a very substantial opposition to this. Indeed the conclusion of the paper had to be that "legislation would require an act of considerable political courage".[8]

Far from seeing the prosecution of the idea of a multi-racial society, the Spring of 1968 was to find Britain confronted with the necessity of placing new curbs in the way of colored immigration. This became evident almost overnight as hosts of Kenyan Indians and Pakistanis, on being deprived of work permits in that country, began to come to Britain under the aegis of United Kingdom passports, which enabled them to find a loophole in the existing Commonwealth Immigration Act (1963). By way of a rushed measure, whose far from perfect drafting reflects the haste with which it was put through, new restraints were placed on citizens of the United Kingdom and Colonies who hold British passports and want to come to live in Britain.[9]

The new Commonwealth Immigrants Act, which came into force on 2 March, now extends to the above-mentioned categories the restraints which previously applied only to other Commonwealth citizens wanting to live in Britain. The only exceptions are those who have a specified connection with Britain, or who have a parent or grandparent of either sex who has had such a connection in the past. Children under sixteen years of age are entitled to be admitted in future only where both parents, or the surviving parent, have been admitted, and any restrictions as to length of stay or employment imposed on the father may be applied equally to wives and children. It is now an offense for a Commonwealth citizen subject to immigration control to land in Britain unless he has been examined by an immigration officer, or lands for examination under approved arrangements.

From the moment of its first appearance—in Bill form—there

has been no dearth of critics who have underlined the many snags in this measure. For one thing, it cannot fully be implemented by Britain without some cooperation from both Kenya and India. At present there seems little hope of the kind of cooperation required being forthcoming. Kenya has decided not to allow holders of British passports to return, while India will not let them in. A peculiarly difficult situation could possibly arise for English settlers in Kenya if that country should decide to withdraw their work permits. Then there would be question of Britain's debarring people of English rather than of Indian ancestry. At the other end of the scale, there seems to exist a loophole for entry by Kenyan Asians under the pretext of coming to holiday in Britain—for there is no restriction against this and no visas required—and at the end of the holiday announcing that they do not wish to leave. The government would be unable to deport them. It is true that, as the law now stands, they would be debarred from working, as they would have no valid work permits. But it is quite likely that very many of them would eventually be placed by those immigrant Asians who have successfully opened businesses in Britain.

Undoubtedly the most fundamental point of criticism of the new Act is that it willy-nilly recreated a racialist atmosphere in Britain. The fact that citizens of the Irish Republic were excluded from its provisions made it ever so much more difficult for its defenders to maintain that its preoccupations were simply with the number of immigrants and not with their origins. Indeed it pulled the carpet from under the Labor Party concept of a multi-racial society. This was the concept that had defeated Gordon Walker in Smethwick in 1964. True, it was temporarily abandoned in 1965—following the elections—when an 8,500 limit on Commonwealth immigrants was imposed by a government White Paper slipped out at the end of the mid-year parliamentary term. By September, however, one found a substantial opposition to the White Paper's provisions developing on the part of a small but influential group of Labour M.P.s.[10] People like Shirley Williams and Michael Foot put out a strongly-worded though restrained document expressing concern at the newly imposed restrictions on immigration and deploring the missed opportunity to liberalize the 1962 Act. They found some support among members of the Liberal Party, among Conservatives like Norman St. John-Stevas and, needless to say, among the supporters of CARD. The last-mentioned were quick to take advantage of what seemed to be the most favorable climate of opinion for their views since their foundation.

Is it any wonder that people like these feel seriously disillusioned by the new Commonwealth Immigrants Act, 1968? More than one of them has declared this to be a clear indication of the impossibility of trying to have things both ways, viz., the specific limitation of colored immigration while claiming to establish a multi-racial society.

Despite this, indeed perhaps because it is an unpalatable truth, the British government is currently preparing new legislation for the improvement of the 1965 Race Relations Act. A secret Home Office memorandum—whose contents were leaked by *The Sunday Times* in March—proposes that damages should be paid to victims of discrimination in employment, housing, insurance and credit facilities and that the Race Relations Board should have comprehensive power to take offenders to a special Court. New voluntary employer-worker machinery to deal quickly with alleged discrimination in employment is suggested.[11]

That these proposals need amendment is the contention of the body known as Equal Rights. Amongst the suggested amendments are that the Race Relations Board should have power to subpoena witnesses, that the special courts should be able to make "stop" orders if an allegation of discrimination has been made, that the Race Relations Board should not have a monopoly of the decision to institute proceedings and that the principle that a racial balance should be maintained within firms should not suffice for refusal of employment to colored workers.[12]

There is undoubtedly some room for more effective legislative action for the eradication of racial discrimination and race prejudice. As far as the latter is concerned, insofar as it is quite frequently an unconscious matter, the legal declaration that something is unlawful can help to erase the attitudes which produce it. In the field of employment there is certainly need for some measure whereby colored applicants will not be turned away without further investigation, as the PEP report showed can happen all too often. At the same time, there should be no gainsaying the fact that, like all immigrants to all countries, colored immigrants to Britain can reasonably expect no more than the right to start at the bottom of the ladder. In housing, the law might well seek to accord equal treatment to colored people in respect of all services that are meant by their nature to be available to everybody. Indeed, the Race Relations Bill has recently been amended, in response to representations made to the Home Secretary, in such a way as to empower the Race Relations Board to require a proved discriminator to sign a written undertaking that he will in future give equal opportunities to colored people. Damages will be available to a victim of discrimination not only for direct loss—as a result for instance of being denied a particular job or house—but also for loss of opportunity.

While it is much to be hoped that Britain will find ways and means of providing a better legislative framework within which her native white majority and immigrant colored minority will live in peace, events during the past few summers in the U.S.A., now most unhappily brought to boiling point by the assassination of Dr. Martin Luther King, proclaim all too clearly that a good legislative integument is not enough. Most of the obvious civil rights victories have been won and there is little more to legislate about in this respect. And yet—during the long, hot summers of 1966 and 1967—what Patrick O'Donovan has described as "a primitive cry of rage without formulated demands" welled up from the ever more progressively Negro urban centers of America.[13]

However, since the Summer of 1967, these demands, as formulated by their more extreme representatives, have become more explicit. But now, with the assassination of Dr. King, the uncontrolled fury that so damages the legitimate pursuit of equal rights is likely to color all the more fiercely the primary need to negotiate for them. To Dr. King not only ends but also means were important. And as he chose to demonstrate the Negro's moral right to equality by attempting to apply the Christian teachings to which large sections of white society paid lip service, then it seems reasonable to conclude that it was the very unassailability of his position, his evident moral superiority over his enemies, that attracted the particular hatred, and now its ultimate release, that people harbor who themselves feel both fear and guilt.

The Summer of 1966 saw riots in twenty cities; twelve dead; three hundred and sixty-six injured; and one thousand, six hundred and forty-seven arrested. That of 1967 saw these respective figures jump to twenty-four; seventy-four; two thousand, one hundred and twenty-two; and four thousand, nine hundred and thirty.

As far as can be discovered—as witness the report on the question to the President submitted by the special National Advisory Commission on Civil Disorders—the trouble has been due mainly to the alienation of the Negro ghettoes (with their disproportionately high quotas of slums and poverty) that represent the open sores of American urban life. It is true that an investigation by Wayne State University psychologists of some four hundred persons arrested during the 1967 Detroit riots has shown that "this was not a poverty riot, this was a protest riot" (for 70% of the rioters had jobs and were averaging 115 dollars a week).[14] Nevertheless, it seems to have been a protest because of the poverty, or rather the generally under-privileged conditions of the Negro in American society. As *Newsweek* has put it: "The marches and the sit-ins and the triumphs of the past had sealed the Negro American's dignity into law—without materially altering the hard, bread-and-butter conditions of his life".[15] Hence the practical policy formulated by the militant, though non-violent Martin Luther King: "Our nettlesome task is to discover how to organize our strength into compelling power so that government cannot elude our demands".[16]

There is no need to catalog the many ways in virtue of which the Negro American still remains submerged. They have been expounded in a wide variety of places.[17] *The Sunday Times'* "Insight" feature (for 30 July, 1967) summed up its investigation of the matter by saying that: "One in three of the Negroes in most Northern cities are unemployed, or as good as unemployed (according to the latest Department of Labor survey); Thirteen years after the Supreme Court outlawed it, there is more segregation in the schools than ever before; In a period of unparalleled boom, after six years of steady economic expansion, median incomes in the urban ghettoes (where most Negroes live) have decreased during the 1960's."

In part, of course, the problem is specifically an urban problem as much as a Negro problem. The American Negroes are flocking to the city centers, finding accommodation in buildings vacated by whites who are moving to the suburbs—so much so that the *Congressional Quarterly* has estimated that by 1970 at least fourteen core-cities will have populations more than 40% black, as have Washington, Baltimore and Detroit already. Urban living can breed problems for people of any color, particularly the urban life of the twentieth century. But there is more to the Negro revolt than that. As *Newsweek* said of the

Detroit riot of 1967: "It was the revolt of the underground, tragically far beyond the ken of most whites and many middle class Negroes. In a crisis mood four top leaders of the Negro establishment [including the late Martin Luther King] put together a statement decrying the riots. . . . But they were the old soldiers of the Negro revolt; the cruel irony of their position today was that the very victories they had won had only quickened Negro hopes—not satisfied them. Revolts are born of hope, not utter despair. . . . "[18]

The more desperate tactics of those whom the same issue of *Newsweek* called "the Jacobins of the ghetto revolution" tend to supplant those that were preferred by Martin Luther King. Floyd McKissick, the angry leader of CORE (Congress of Racial Equality) predicts hotter summers to come unless basic changes are made in the black man's place in America and the according to him of real economic and political power.[19] Rap Brown, who has taken over leadership of SNCC (the Student Non-Violent Co-ordinating Committee) from Stokely Carmichael, has a simple prescription, even if it is one that contradicts the title of his movement: "Black folks built America, and if America don't come around we're going to burn America down."[20] Not surprisingly, the Black Panther movement has named Carmichael Prime Minister of their shadow government and Brown its Minister for Justice.

As far as Britain is concerned, there is a real possibility that even if colored immigrants are accorded the most impeccable legal conditions they will become ever more restive until they are fully integrated. This would mean not only more and better jobs, housing and general politico-social conditions but—ultimately— even the likelihood of miscegenation. Whether a country should set out to create a multi-racial society that would inevitably come eventually to demand this, or whether it might not be better advised to try to carve out a simpler destiny, is a question that only future history will fully answer.

Notes

1. Cf. "A Hardening Colour Bar—The Law", in *New Society*, 16 March 1967.

2. R. B. Davison, *Black British*, London, 1967.

3. *New Society*, 16 March, 1967.

4. Dipak Nandy, "Discrimination: The Ugly Facts", in *New Statesman*, 21 April, 1967.

5. Cf. David Knox, "*Michael X*", in *Life*, 16 October, 1967.

6. *Ibid.*

7. Cf. series of articles in *The Times*, 11–15 March, 1968. Cf. also "Mainspring of Black Power"—Colin McGlashan interview with Stokely Carmichael, in *The Observer*, 23 July, 1967.

8. Cf. *Sunday Times*, 7 May, 1967.

9. Cf. *The Sunday Times*, 3 March, 1968.

10. Cf. David Leitch, "The Race Rebels", in *The Sunday Times*, 26 September, 1965.

11. Cf. *The Sunday Times*, 3 March, 1968.

12. Cf. *The Sunday Times*, 10 March, 1968.

13. Cf. Patrick O'Donovan, "Hope Out of the Hatred", in *The Observer*, 22 August, 1965.

14. Cf. *Newsweek*, 11 March, 1968, p. 10.

15. *Newsweek*, 15 May, 1967, "Which Way for the Negro Now?"

16. *Ibid.*

17. E.g. "What the Negro has and has not Gained", in *Time*, 28 October, 1966: "The Negro in America: What Must be Done", in *Newsweek* (Special Issue), 20 November, 1967: W. J. Weatherby, "Summer on the Harlem Wall", in *New Society*, 12 July, 1967.

18. *Newsweek*, 7 August, 1967.

19. Cf. Evelyn Irons in *The Sunday Times*, 21 May, 1967.

20. Cf. *Newsweek*, 7 August, 1967.

For Further Reading

Ronald Segal, *The Race War*, London, 1967.

The Natoinal Advisory Commission on Civil Disorders: Report, Washington, 1968.

PEP Report on Racial Discrimination, London, 1967.

CHAPTER I

Problems of Race and Migration

What is called the "race question" is undeniably one of the biggest problems of the middle decades of the twentieth century. In one way or another it has cropped up in all five continents. Racial segregation, racial discrimination and simple race prejudice are to be found under a great variety of forms. Very frequently they are practical by-products of interracial conflict, but most often they are intermixed with theories concerning racial superiority and inferiority.

Race and Exaggerated Nationalism

However widespread the question of race may be in its direct manifestations, its indirect effects are even more varied and complex. One of the most far-reaching of these is its role in stimulating exaggerated nationalism, or at least a nationalism that takes little or no account of the organic nature of international society as a whole. There are many examples—some more extreme than others—of the identification of racial and national interests.[1] They are to be found among the ideas of otherwise widely divergent thinkers.

It was a French writer—and a prominent Roman Catholic at that—who propounded one of the most biased concepts of nationalism and its implications based on a close association of nationality and race. "Nations," wrote Joseph de Maistre, "are born and die like individuals . . .; they have a common soul" and should try to remain "frankly of one race."[2] The German phil-

osopher Hegel had a similar concept of a racial soul: "The differences of races is a natural difference, that is, one regarding the
natural soul."[3] Even those who do try to distinguish between
"race" and "nation" and to keep the implications of each
separate, all too easily find themselves effecting the opposite to
what they wish. Such, for example, was André Suarès, who
maintained that "a nation is a spirit" whereas "a race is the
corporeal form of a nation."[4] This approach merely distinguishes
in order the better to unite, *distinguer pour mieux unir*, to use
the expression of Jacques Maritain.

The most theoretically extensive and practically effective link-
ing of nationality and race was accomplished by the Nazi philosopher and propagandist Alfred Rosenberg (1893–1946). In the
Vossische Zeitung of September 3, 1933 he made one of his most
forceful statements on the subject:

> A nation is constituted by the predominance of a definite character
> formed by its blood, also by language, geographical environment,
> and the sense of a united political destiny. These last constituents
> are not, however, definitive; the decisive element in a nation is its
> blood. In the first awakening of a people, great poets and heroes
> disclose themselves to us as the incorporation of the eternal values
> of a particular blood soul. I believe that this recognition of the
> profound significance of blood is now mysteriously encircling our
> planet, irresistibly gripping one nation after another.

It was Rosenberg's view that when Martin Luther opposed his
idea of national states to the world domination of the papacy, he
was fighting against a "chaos of races." Proper order, he argued,
demands a racial-national system of individuation. In accordance
with this, Adolf Hitler placed before National Socialism the
supreme task of creating a new "Teutonic state of German
nationality."[5] It was this that brought him into early conflict
both with international Jewry and the internationalism of Marxist
Communism. "The Jewish doctrine of Marxism," he wrote in
Mein Kampf, "rejects the aristocratic principle of nature and puts

in place of the eternal privilege of power and strength the mass and the dead weight of number. Thus it denies in mankind the value of Personality, contests the significance of Nationality and Race, and so withdraws from men the essential foundation of their existence and their culture."[6]

In the Rosenberg-Hitler system it is hard to be sure which was the hen and which the egg, nationalism or the racism with which it was associated. All that can be said with certainty is that racism was an integral part of National Socialism and its attendant consequences. But there are other and indisputable examples of racism giving birth to a similar nationalism. One of the best-known is the "Black Nationalist" movement in the United States.

This movement goes back to the years immediately following World War I, when Marcus Garvey called on Negro Americans to return to Africa. Because of its powerful emotional appeal, his Universal Negro Improvement Association soon attained mass dimensions, some 300,000 Negro Americans enrolling in it or contributing towards its objective—the establishment of an African state to be populated by black American emigrés. Yet this "Back to Africa" movement was doomed to failure from the start "because," as Martin Luther King has put it, "an exodus by a people who had struck roots for three and a half centuries in the New World did not have the ring of progress."[7]

The Garvey movement is not the only manifestation of black nationalism stimulated by racism. In addition to it, the United States has seen the emergence of The Peace Movement of Ethiopia, The National Union for People of African Descent, The National Movement for the Establishment of the Forty-Ninth State, and the Black Muslim Movement.[8] It is true that some of these have been influenced by the contemporary rise of new black nations in Africa. But it is likely that in all cases—and particularly that of the Black Muslims—the main reason for their appearance has been the lack of hope that racial justice will ever be achieved in the United States. Indeed the center of the Black

Muslim position is that an interracial society based on justice is an impossibility.[9] Urging a permanent and complete separation of the races, the Black Muslims differ from Garvey's followers in that they appear to believe that this can be achieved better in America than by going to Africa. Although they seem to have only a fractional support in the American Negro community, they show what racism can do toward encouraging a nationalist isolationism.

The Summer of 1966 saw the re-emergence in America of racist nationalism under the new slogan of "Black Power." Originally used as a rallying cry during the "Meredith march" through Mississippi in June, and possessing no very clear meaning, by July it had been defined by a resolution emanating from the Congress of Racial Equality as "self-determination by men of color in their own areas." As such it was declared by the resolution to be "simply what all other groups in American society have done to acquire their share of the total wealth." In short, it meant a proportionate control of the "economic, political, educational, and social wealth of our community from top to bottom."

But it is susceptible to more extreme formulations. One such, which appeared in a paper prepared by Stokely Carmichael, leader of the Student Non-Violent Committee, declared: "If we are to proceed towards liberation, then we must cut ourselves off from the white people . . . We propose that our organization should be black-staffed, black-controlled and black-financed. If we continue to rely upon white financial support we will find ourselves entwined in the tentacles of the white-power complex which controls this country."[10]

Even more radical interpretation has been given to the phrase by the Black Muslims. The Black Muslim leader, Elijah Muhamad, told his five thousand followers in Chicago that "the white man is the enemy of God, of human beings and of himself. We hate the white man. We gave him the power to rule over us and we can take it away. This is not a white man's world . . . I say to the white man, it is our time and we shall rule." Reminding his followers that there are twenty-seven Muslim countries and more than six hundred million Muslims, he pointed out that "there are eleven of us to one of him [i.e., the white man] in the world. If we have unity, what can that one do? That is black power."[11]

In this context racism assumes the character of a militant internationalism more extreme in nature than any exaggerated racist nationalism.

At the other end of the scale, there have been over the course of history abundant examples of racist-nationalism conducing to colonial expansionism. Jacques Barzun has propounded a thesis that racial hegemony provides the key to an understanding of the imperialistic phases of the various nations of Europe.[12] It has played its part, too, in the arguments between states about subject nationalities, boundary lines and the like. (Inversely, during a period of contraction in the fortunes of France, it has been used in the Dreyfus affair to attribute the ills of the nation to infection due to the Jewish racial strain.) No people can claim to be entirely free from at least colonial dreams in the name of, and for the expansion of, its stock. The classical statement of this was formulated about the year 1900 in the *Last Will and Testament* of Cecil Rhodes: "The furtherance of the British Empire for the bringing of the whole uncivilized world under British rule, for the recovery of the United States, for the making of the Anglo-Saxon race but one empire. What a dream! And yet it is probable. It is possible."

Race and Migration Restriction

An important consequence of racism—whether directly or under the aegis of a nationalism inspired by it—is the restriction of freedom of movement and of migration. The link between racist thinking and these restrictions was painfully apparent in Rosenberg's program for a post-war Europe. He had always seen the primary aim of German policy as the securing of territory for settlement and the creation of a large and strong German Central Europe which would ensure the domination of the white race throughout the world. From this hypothesis he drew an immediate inference bearing on migration: "Just as it will be necessary to put an end to individual freedom of movement in Germany in order to prevent an agglomeration of people in the large cities, in order to prevent racial cross-breeding it will be necessary to eliminate from the Nordic State all racially different elements such as Negroes, Mongols and Jews."[13]

To secure the first of these objectives the Reich Hereditary Farm Laws of September 29, 1933 were passed. In an effort to keep the people on the land, estates which were able to provide a living for a family were converted by these laws into hereditary entities which could neither be mortgaged nor sold by their owners. The securing of the second objective was at least partially effected by the elimination of the Jews; the question of the Negroes and the Mongols did not arise in practice. But it is only too clear that a restriction, if not a total barring, of the migration of these people to (Central) Europe would have been an integral part of the racial policy of the Hitler régime.

Everybody knows of the extremism of this policy. What is not sufficiently realized is the influence racism has had on countries not customarily accused of racist thinking. This is true, for example, of the migration restrictions that are part and parcel of the American scene. This is clearly implied by the fact that the movement towards the restriction of immigration into the United States came after a great increase in immigration from 1880 on, coupled with a shift in its source from Northern to South Eastern Europe.[14] In his book on the subject, the late President John F. Kennedy noted that the new restrictions represented a "social and economic reaction" to these facts.[15] The term "social" here without doubt covers "racial" also. The 1924 Immigration Act, which determined the quotas for annual immigration from each sending country, was veiledly but unmistakably racist in undertone. Indeed in the preface to his book, *The Passing of the Great Race*,[16] a prominent American racist, Madison Grant (1865–1937), openly boasted that it was under the influence of his book that Congress passed the new law, "the object of which is to bar undesirable races and peoples from the U.S.A."

President Kennedy made no attempt to deny the presence of this racial element. He wrote: "Because of the composition of our population in 1920, the system is heavily weighted in favor of immigration from Northern Europe and severely limits immigration from Southern and Eastern Europe and from other parts of the world."[17] He drew attention to one writer's analysis of the motives for the 1924 measure as including post-war isolation and a fear of pauper labor and of foreign ideologies, but also a belief in the superiority of the Anglo-Saxon and Teutonic races. Speaking himself of this Act—and of its successor, the Immigration and Nationality Act, 1952—President Kennedy declared that "the national origins quota system has strong overtones of an indefensible racial prejudice."[18] Of the same Act, former President Harry S. Truman said: "The idea behind this discriminatory policy was, to put it boldly, that Americans with English or Irish names were better people and better citizens than Americans with Italian or Greek or Polish names. . . ."[19]

Nor is America alone in having such racist-influenced immigration control. The whole problem of the north of Australia is bound up with the thorny "White Australia" policy. We will return later to a close examination of this policy, as well as of the present immigration restrictions in force in Britain.

What we wish to point out here is that migration controls that are inspired by racist thinking or race prejudice can themselves be a substantial cause of racial discrimination and of a race problem in general in a country. This was the burden of Dr.

Martin Luther King's remarks when, during the course of his visit to England in December, 1964, he warned Britain against allowing a serious racial situation to develop in the years ahead. He said that immigration laws based on color would "eventually encourage the vestiges of racism" and endanger Britain's democratic principles.[20]

Perhaps it is not to be wondered at that, as a series of articles on the color problem in Britain first pointed out in January, 1965, awful generalizations about color are beginning to be heard in Britain, such as the attributing of this, that or the other socially undesirable trait to colored people.[21] It is amazing how widespread are these prejudiced attitudes; they are partaken of by the most educated people, including prominent members of the Christian churches. The London *Times* could report, for example, that a vicar writing from near Ross-on-Wye to a newspaper at Leyton said that colored people should be given return tickets to their own countries.[22]

Contrariwise, there has always been a problem arising from the presence of white migrant minorities in colonial areas. Miss Margery Perham believes that emigration from the colonizing countries has ever been, by its very nature, the greatest challenge to Christian and philanthropic attempts to protect the rights of the native peoples. For however humane the colonial policy of the metropolitan power may be, it can be countered by measures emanating from new centers of politics set up by the emigrants themselves. "So the theme of disputed power runs beside that of disputed morality, and we can trace this conflict also, certainly from Roman days, to the recent tragic events in Algeria, and again, to those which have faced Britain in East and Central Africa."[23] The situation in Southern Rhodesia is a case in point. Thus Charles Olley, former mayor of Salisbury, called for white immigration on a gigantic scale: "As the natives are so far behind, it is imperative that there shall be white supremacy for hundreds of years . . . Actually it is not their [i.e. the natives'] country; in fact, less so than that of Europeans from the point of view of [being] conquered territory."[24]

In one form or another—whether by way of breeding either exaggerated and isolationist nationalism or an expansionist colonialism—one finds the race question frequently at the root of migration problems, particularly those caused by the restriction of migration. So close indeed is the interrelation between race and migration problems that it would seem to be an *a priori* probability that an understanding of the one should throw some light on the other when there is question of framing national policies. In the following chapters we shall examine various aspects of each in the hope that some such light may emerge.

Notes

1. Cf. Thomas Franck, *Race and Nationalism* (London, 1960), *passim*.

2. *Considerations sur la France*. Cited in Jacques Barzun, *Race: A Study in Modern Superstition* (London, 1938).

3. *Philosophy of Mind*. Cited in Barzun, *op. cit.*, p. 62.

4. *La Nation contre la Race*, 2 vols. (Paris, 1916-1917).

5. Cited in Irene Marinoff, *The Heresy of National Socialism* (London, 1941), p. 71.

6. Cited in Marinoff, *op. cit.*, p. 38.

7. Martin Luther King, *Why We Can't Wait* (New York, 1963), p. 33.

8. Cf. Gunnar Myrdal, *An American Dilemma: The Negro Problem and Modern Democracy* (New York, 1962), p. 812 seq.

9. Cf. John A. Morsell, "Black Nationalism," in *The Catholic Mind*, LXI (1963).

10. As reported in *The Observer* of London, August 28, 1966.

11. As reported in the Dublin *Evening Press*, August 29, 1966.

12. Barzun, *op. cit.* Cf. his chapters on "Race and Nationalistic Wars."

13. Cited in Marinoff, *op. cit.*, pp. 80–81.

14. Cf. Chapter VII, below, p. 121 ff.

15. *A Nation of Immigrants* (New York, 1964), p. 74.

16. New York, 1916.

17. *Op. cit.*, p. 75.

18. *Op. cit.*, p. 77.

19. Cited in Kennedy, *op. cit.*, p. 78.

20. As reported in *The Irish Independent*, December 7, 1964.

21. Cf. "The Dark Million," in *The Times* of London, January 28, 1965.

22. *Loc. cit.*

23. Margery Perham, *The Colonial Reckoning* (London, 1963), p. 82.

24. Cited in Patrick Keatley, *The Politics of Partnership: The Federation of Rhodesia and Nyasaland* (London, 1963), p. 263.

For Further Reading

E. W. Count, *This is Race*, New York, 1950. Contains extracts from the main publications on race for two hundred years.

E. U. Essien–Udom, *Black Nationalism: The Rise of the Black Muslims in the U.S.A.*, Chicago, 1962.

J. Carlton Hayes, *Historical Evolution of Modern Nationalism*, New York, 1931.

Geoffrey M. Morant, "Racial Theories and International Relations," in *Journal of the Royal Anthropological Institute*, vol. 69 (1939), pp. 151–162.

J. Oakeswith, *Race and Nationalism*, New York, 1919.

Sir Herbert Samuel, *Wars of Ideas*, London, 1937. An account of modern racist, especially German, ideas.

Boyd C. Shaefer, *Nationalism*, London, 1955.

A. P. Thornton, *Doctrines of Imperialism*, New York, 1965.

CHAPTER II

The Meaning of Race

The term race seems to have been first introduced by Count George Louis Buffon (1707–1788). As originally used it did not have any very precise meaning. It was employed to cover different broad sections of mankind, the members of each respective section bearing a certain resemblance to one another while differing markedly from the members of the other sections. This division was effected merely on the basis of common observation and was therefore bound to be vague.

However, it did result in a division of mankind into what were called the great and the lesser races. Examples of the great races were Europeans in general, Negroes in general, Asiatics in general. The lesser races or ethnic groups, on the other hand, were sub-divisions of each of the great races. For example, Europeans were divided into Nordic, Alpine and Mediterranean.

Soon, for military and political reasons, the popular idea grew up—encouraged by some scholars[1]—that further sub-divisions of race existed, as between the respective populations of at least the great European States. Thus one began to hear of the Gallic race, centered in France, the Aryan race, centered in Germany, and the British race centered in England.

Gradually, as a more scientific anthropology developed, efforts at a more accurate classification of races were made. The working definition of race which was used for this purpose was that put forward in 1859 by Armand de Quatrefages who described race as "a totality of similar individuals."[2] This working definition, or better, working hypothesis, has continued to be employed into the present century. Thus in 1928 Rudolf Martin wrote: "Individuals belonging to one race have a certain number of characteristics in common, the combination of which distinguishes them from other groups."[3] But the big question which has always confronted the scientists has been, what are the characteristics which differentiate racial types?

The Difficulty of Racial Classification

Mental traits. The first classification of the races to be attempted on a scientific basis was that made by Linnaeus (Carl von Linné, 1707–1777) in 1738.[4] The criterion used was that of mental traits. From this system emerged four racial types—*Homo Americanus, Homo Europaeus, Homo Asiaticus* and *Homo Afer.* American man was described as being tenacious, contented, free and ruled by custom. European man, on the other hand, was said to be light, lively, inventive and ruled by rites. Asiatic man was said to be stern, haughty, stingy and ruled by opinion, while African man was cunning, slow, negligent and ruled by caprice.

This classification found a considerable degree of support during the eighteenth century due to the prevailing materialism with its mechanical notion of mind. Philosophers such as Pierre Cabanis (1757–1808) believed in an exact correspondence between mind and body of a kind which made racial classification by way of mental traits eminently intelligible. This approach, however, was quickly abandoned, not only because of a fear on the part of the more orthodox philosophers of tampering with the soul of man, but because of the scientific difficulties with which it was inherently confronted. The fact is that the traits in question are widely distributed among all populations. (See Dunn and Dobzhansky, *Heredity, Race and Society*, New York, 1957).

It is evident, of course, that human experience over the course of time must play a considerable role in the development of the nervous system, and, since this is transmitted by heredity, it

would not at all be surprising if different mental traits were to be
found among populations whose spatio-temporal backgrounds
were different. Be this as it may, it has never been demonstrated
that in different human ethnic groups the nervous system differs
in any of its structural characters.[5] Even should it be found that
it does, it still remains certain that the differences would be of the
most insignificant kind. Furthermore, the mental differences
which exist between human groups appear to be much less than
those which are found between individuals of the same group.
The upshot of it all is that it is entirely unprofitable to seek a
scientific classification of the races on the basis of mental traits.
One anthropologist has summed up the position as follows:
"Since mental functions are so largely dependent upon experience, upon cultural conditions, it is impossible to make any
inferences as to the equivalence or non-equivalence of mental
potentialities as between races or peoples among whom the
cultural conditions are not strictly comparable."[6]

Skin pigmentation. A second attempt at classification, based on
the pigmentation of the skin, was made in 1764 by Louis Jean
Daubenton (1716–1799). This classification, which is usually
attributed to Johann Friedrich Blumenbach writing around 1775,[7]
yielded five great races of mankind. These were the white or
Caucasian, the black or Ethiopian, the yellow or Mongolian, the
red or American, and the brown or Malayan races. But these
efforts were also abandoned in face of difficulties. It was pointed
out, first of all, that there are really many different shades of
color among individuals who are known to have the same genetic
constitution. Europeans, for example, range from a pale pink
among the Nordic and Alpine people to a dark brown among the
Mediterranean. In like manner, Africans and Asians go from
pale yellow to a swarthy black. Secondly, it was noted that the
same color of skin can sometimes be found in individuals who are
known to possess different genetic constitutions. Hence skin

color does not make for either fundamental unity or fundamental diversity. Finally, there was the consideration that skin pigmentation in itself depends largely on the mechanical action of environment.

This last point would not have bothered the original defenders of the skin pigmentation theory. For early nineteenth-century anthropologists regarded race as the product of the mechanical action of environment. The effect of environment on skin pigmentation was only one of the examples which they used to cite. Many other differences were attributed to it also.[8] Thus Andreas Vesalius (1513–1564) maintained that the different forms of the cranium observable among peoples are due to their different ways of cradling infants.[9] This environmental school continues to have adherents right up to the present day.[10] J. L. Myres, writing in 1923, declared that Mongoloid facial traits are due at least partly to the fact that infants are suckled by mares.[11] K. Davies, in 1932, saw the slit nose of the Eskimo as the fruit of nature's adaptation to climate, this characteristic being advantageous for the intake of cold air.[12] In the same way, I. Semenov, as recently as 1951, declared that the peculiar eyes of the Berbers constitute a defense against light and wind.[13]

The vast majority of modern anthropologists, however, confine the mechanical influence of environment to the production of rapid modifications of characteristics which do not pertain to the idea of race. They have been compelled to do this by certain facts. Thus, a Mongoloid group transplanted into a new geographical setting will increase in stature yet remain clearly Mongoloid. So, too, an Irishman remains distinctively European even though he may become brown from the sun in certain conditions. Hence skin pigmentation in itself was abandoned relatively quickly as an adequate criterion for race classification.

Physical Measurements. The next criterion put forward was that of physical measurements. These pertained especially to the shape and size of the head, though they were usually taken in conjunction with other considerations such as skin pigmentation, the shape of the nose, the lips, the eyes, the type of hair and the color of the eyes.

Physical measurements resulted in no uniform classification. We find J. Deniker, in 1889, arriving at 30 races on the basis of them,[14] while E. Von Eickstedt, in 1933, defended the existence of three basic races, 18 sub-races, three collateral races, 11 collateral sub-races and three intermediate forms.[15] More recently, in 1950, C. S. Coon, S. M. Garn and J. B. Birdsell held for the existence of what they called six putative stocks and 30 races.[16]

This complexity has made it increasingly clear that these criteria of racial classification concern only what is called the racial phenotype. As such they do not go deep enough. What must be sought is the genotype, th?t is, typological characteristics stemming from gene compositions. In other words, it is necessary to look for fundamental rather than merely externally observable differences, for biological rather than simple somatic characteristics.

Blood composition. Recent efforts to do this have been made on the basis of the composition of the blood,[17] to determine whether races correspond to any of the well defined blood groups—O, A, B, and AB. The blood groups of people in all parts of the world have been studied, but no clear-cut boundaries between the different "races" on the basis of blood groupings have been found. There is a great deal of mixture and overlapping. Blood group O, for example, is found among every people ; blood group A is also common.

The most that can be said in the direction of classification is that the respective blood groups are found to be present in different proportions among different populations. Thus, between 90 percent and 100 percent of American Indians belong to blood group O, whereas only 50 percent of the population of England belong to it. Similarly, the proportions of populations belonging to blood groups A and B increase as one moves eastward across Europe, blood group A increasing from Iceland to Russia, and blood group B from Finland to Siberia. On the other hand, it has been found that while group B is predominant in Central Asia and Siberia, it is absent in the aboriginal population of Australia and very little of it is to be found among the Eskimos.

Thus blood grouping, no more than the other criteria which have been put forward, does not provide an absolute basis for the classification of the races. Says one authority: "It cannot be too emphatically or too often repeated that fundamentally the blood of all human beings is similar no matter what class, group, nation or race they belong to." And again: "There are no demonstrable or known differences but statistical ones in the character of the blood of different peoples. In that sense the biblical *obiter dictum* that the Lord 'hath made of one blood all nations of men to dwell on the face of the earth' is literally true."[18]

In any case genotypic differences related to the composition of the blood could never be positively correlated with phenotypic differences. For blood in itself is in no way connected with the transmission of the hereditary characters.[19] That it was so connected seems to have been linked in the past with the idea that the blood of the mother is transmitted to the child. This is now known to be incorrect. The mother does not contribute blood to the foetus; rather the developing child manufactures its own blood. For this reason claims to kinship based on the specific tie of blood have no scientific foundation, as neither have claims to a common group consciousness derived from a common blood. The character of the blood of all human beings is essentially a human rather than a national or group product.

Two main points emerge from our investigation. Firstly, it is not possible to draw up an absolutely distinct classification of races. Secondly, it is possible to arrive at a vague classification of races in terms of frequency, that is, the frequency with which a certain type of blood composition turns up in individuals over certain broad areas of the world. This is the most that can be done by way of the isolation of genotypes.

In so far as this is so, race is a statistical concept, a combination of averages—in other words, an abstraction. It is essentially something that applies only to groups as a whole and not to any particular individual within these groups.[20] This is something that is clearly of practical as well as of scientific import. And although the credit for the discovery is usually given to the French anthropologist Paul Topinard, who published his *Anthropologie Générale* in Paris in 1885, it was first advanced by an Irishman, the Belfast apothecary John Grattan, in the 1850's.[21]

All this means that scientists have not gone far toward a numerically rigid classification of distinct races. A European, for example, might safely get a blood transfusion from a Negro of the same blood grouping yet die from a transfusion from a European of a different grouping. This means that there are no such things as pure races, something which has been recognized by anthropologists since the end of the last century. It was Topinard who said: "We are all half-breeds."[22]

Did Pure Races Ever Exist?

Yet just as surely anthropologists have tended to believe that there were pure races (primary races) in existence at one time although they are now intermixed by cross-breeding, and that this cross-breeding itself could in time beget new pure races (secondary races), indeed that it is now, in fact, in the process of doing so.

Such beliefs are unfounded. For one thing, the primary races in question are purely hypothetical entities, which are assumed rather than proved to have once existed. There is no evidence for their ever having existed. On the contrary, what evidence there is, is that ancient populations were just as mixed as are present-day ones. This has been deduced from the examination of skeletal remains two to six thousand years old. "Hence," says the American anthropologist Raymond Firth, "to embark on discussions regarding the inter-mixture of a number of hypothetical pure stocks is unprofitable, and there is no direct evidence whatever for the existence of 'pure' racial populations."[23]

As recently as 1962, however, the anthropologist Carleton S. Coon put forward the view that mankind (*Homo Sapiens*) comprises five highly distinct sub-species, the Australoid, Caucasoid, Mongoloid, Congoid (African-Negroes and Pygmies) and Capoid (Bushmen and Hottentots), which sub-species have developed separately over a long period and have in fact each a separate ancestry from a more primitive stage of development.[24] In Coon's opinion, *Homo Erectus* evolved into *Homo Sapiens* not once but five times, as each sub-species, living in its own territory, passed a critical threshold from a more brutal to a more sapient state. He adds that the Capoid and Australoid types of hominid later each produced a people of hereditary dwarfs, the Pygmies and the Negritos respectively, who together with the five original subspecies form the seven races of Man. In accordance with this approach, Professor Coon believes that genetic variations favoring more complex social and cultural behavior arose independently in several places and spread by way of natural selection in virtue of the advantages which they conferred. But certain isolated peoples, he believes, as in Nether Africa and Australasia, were late in receiving these benefits and therefore lag behind the people of Europe and Asia.

This view—that the human species, because of the separate evolution of its different branches, is polytypic—has been termed a "doctrine of evolutionary apartheid,"[25] which would be very easy for men of ill-will to use to justify racial discrimination in the name of science. Admittedly it has certain attractions in other respects. Its theory of cross-breeding provides an easy solution to the present-day difficulties in finding reliable criteria of racial classification.

As a scientific thesis, however, Professor Coon's view has come in for severe criticism. Quite a number of defects in it have been pointed out.[26] The fossil evidence, itself slim in quantity, provides no basis for the theory Professor Coon has erected on it. In particular, it can tell us nothing about non-skeletal factors, whose relevance cannot be ignored. In point of fact, the Bushmen and Hottentots, members of the so-called Capoid sub-species, have been shown by several recent expeditions to be basically Negroid in genetic constitution, despite certain locally evolved differences such as lighter skin color. They are, in fact, light colored Negroids, the fruit of a polymorphic development rather than the result of a polytypic sub-speciation.

Indeed, in place of the polytypic variation between geographically separate breeding populations before the emergence of *Homo Sapiens*, as advanced by Professor Coon, the majority of anthropologists defend a polymorphic interpretation. They maintain that there is no reason why the sub-specific variations of mankind should not have emerged relatively late and represent variations within the unified breeding population of *Homo Sapiens* as he spread and occupied more and variegated territory. Professor V. P. Yakimov, of the Institute of Ethnography in Moscow, has written that "the view that racial differentiation took place comparatively late within the already formed species *Homo Sapiens* . . . seems to us to be biologically sounder."[27] For Professor Coon's theory to be valid it would have been necessary for human evolution to have stopped short in the case of some groups and gone further in the case of others. But the evidence is that the different sections of mankind have been differentiating more or less independently and at the same time.

Could Pure Races Emerge in the Future?

So much, then, for the so-called primary races. What of the possibility of the emergence of pure secondary races? The idea that cross-breeding can be a source of new pure stocks was originally suggested by Quatrefages. It has found a good deal of support in recent times from Coon, Garn and Birdsell, who see in it the possibility that the American Negroes may represent a future new race in the making.[28] Presumably it would also mean that eventually pure Nordic and other races will emerge, particularly if present-day Nordic and other communities are preserved from outside racial influences.

This idea is a myth, for the emergence of such races is biologically impossible. Even if isolated entirely, a people would not develop into a pure race through the process of inter-breeding within itself.[29] The reason lies in the mechanism of heredity by which the most important physical characteristics are transmitted.[30] This mechanism is such that there is not, nor can there be, any certainty that a given characteristic will in fact be transmitted to a given individual. Such certainty would be possible only if heredity were transmitted as in a fluid, in which the characteristics of both parents were contained and mixed perfectly, resulting in an offspring possessing characteristics which represented their common denominator. In fact, however, transmission is by way of discrete packages, the genes, that do not mix thus.[31] No single physical characteristic is transmitted by a single gene, but only by a combination of genes. And there is no guarantee that this combination will necessarily be effected. In addition, genes for one physical characteristic, for example, the type of hair, can be inherited without necessarily being accompanied by genes for other characteristics that usually go with the first, say, for example, the shape of the nose.

Hence intermarriage within an isolated group cannot with certainty create a community in which all the individual members will have exactly the same physical characteristics. The most it could do would be to push the frequencies of the genes that are responsible for the different characteristics towards equality. Thus if at present 90 percent of the members of a community had blue eyes and 10 percent brown eyes, intermarriage over a long period would lead to an increase in the number of brown-eyed individuals, because the number of couples in which one party has blue eyes and the other brown eyes will be greater than if there were no intermarriage, thereby increasing the chances for brown eyes being inherited. And if the intermarriage continued long enough, the tendency would be for the proportions of the blue-eyed and the brown-eyed to become equal. But one would still be left with blue-eyed people and brown-eyed people in the community rather than with a pure blue-brown-eyed race.[32]

Hence the generally held position might be summed up by saying that a pure race is something that cannot be found at the present day, does not seem to have ever existed in the past, and will not emerge in the future.

Race is Something Real but Elusive

While it is true that the different characteristics of mankind merge into one another and that race is a statistical abstraction applying to whole groups rather than to individuals, it must not be thought that there is no extra-mental reality corresponding to the concept "race." To quote two distinguished contemporary anthropologists: "One should not conclude that because the dividing lines between races are frequently arbitrary, races are imaginary entities. By looking at a suburban landscape one cannot always be sure where the sea begins and the country ends, but it does not follow from this that the sea exists only in imagination. Races exist regardless of whether we can easily define them or not."[33] And it was Topinard who wrote: "Race in the present state of things is an abstract conception, the notion of continuity and discontinuity, of unity in diversity. It is the rehabilitation of a real but directly unattainable thing. . . . At the present time rarely, if indeed ever, we discover a single individual corresponding to our racial type in every detail. It exists for us nevertheless."[34]

This is true in a certain broad sense.[35] Thus, in a general way, Europeans are distinguishable from Asiatics, Africans, American Indians and Australoids, and are distinguishable among themselves into Nordic, Alpine and Mediterranean. In this same general context physical characteristics can be used as a basis of classification. This is the approach of Coon, Garn and Birdsell. Similarly, mental traits are associated with race by a number of anthropologists, as, for example, Franz Boas,[36] although they add them only when their classification of races has otherwise been primarily derived. And as physical characteristics particularly are principally caused by environment, maps showing the geographical variation of somatic characteristics are in order and have a restricted validity. We find them used, for example, by Paul Broca[37] and others.

Nevertheless, the precise reality corresponding to the concept of race continues to be the subject of lively controversy between the adherents of typological and populationist thinking.[38] According to the populationists, race is a breeding population, or group of related populations, which differ from other such groupings of the same human species in gene frequencies linked with the occurrence of certain characteristics. The big weakness in this populationist view of the nature of race is that it takes no cognizance of intra-group variability. There is the danger, too, of identifying racial characteristics with the average characteristics of a population, in such a way that the average comes to be identified with the characteristics of the group as a whole and of each of its members.

To avoid this the typologists prefer to speak of the existence of racial elements or types, each element comprising all individuals, no matter from which population they come, who display a certain combination of characteristics. But this view is also confronted with difficulties. The fact that every human population contains several such elements means that races, in so far as they have existence as understood by the typologists, are so widely diffused and intermixed as to have little or no practical relevance. The more fundamental difficulty is that neither phenotypic nor genotypic similarity in separate characteristics, or even in sets of characteristics, ensures any unity of origin or direct kinship between those compared.[39] We are left, therefore, with the fact that the construction of a neat racial classification, with a definite number of races possessing clear-cut boundaries, is a task unfeasible both for the populationist with his statistical averages and the typologist with his nebulous racial elements.

What is quite certain is that no racial type is confined to any particular geographical area or state. It has rightly been said that "the present populations of Europe, America, Africa and Asia are hybrid in the extreme."[40] Racial mixing has occurred even in the case of extremely isolated groups,[41] and even more in the case of populations among whom mixing was easier.[42] The Swedes are regarded as the most Nordic of Europeans. Yet an 1897 investigation of 45,000 soldiers showed that only 11 percent were of the pure Nordic phenotype, characterized by long skulls, tall stature, fair hair and light eyes. Indeed the maximum of such in any province was shown to be only 18.5 percent. A similar investigation made thirty years later reached parallel conclusions.

In the case of the Germans, too, there is a great variety of physical types. They range from Nordic in the North West to Alpine in the South, with many intermediate forms. The Jews are frequently regarded as a separate race. Yet every region of Europe has its own physical type of Jew. In northern Europe 30 percent are blonde, 50 percent have light colored eyes and on the whole they are broad rather than narrow-headed. Non-European Jews vary even more. We find Indian-type, Chinese-type and African-type Jews.

Any rigid taxonomic classification of mankind into distinct races, therefore, is impossible. This conclusion has been confirmed by the Unesco meeting of scientists who gathered in Moscow in August, 1964 to study the biological aspects of race. In the statement which they issued following this meeting,[43] they unanimously agreed that all men living today belong to a single species, *Homo Sapiens*, and are derived from a common stock. They agreed, too, that there is great genetic diversity within all human populations. Pure races, in the sense of genetically homogeneous populations, do not, said the statement, exist in the human species. It added that while different classifications of mankind into major and minor stocks, and maps of their geographical distribution, may have a certain practical utility, they cannot claim to divide mankind into clear-cut categories.

Two final considerations must be added. Firstly, race is as much a social as a biological thing. Biologists themselves are the first to insist that the biological development of man cannot be considered apart from his social development. For example, Dr. R. A. Fischer has said that "while genetic knowledge is essential for the clarity it introduces into the subject, the causes of the evolutionary changes in progress can only be resolved by an appeal to sociological and even historical facts."[44]

The second point is that race is essentially a mutable thing.[45] It is never more than a series of temporary genetic conditions that are always in the process of change. Once this is realized it becomes clear that the stage at which this process is examined is always dependent upon the segment of time which is arbitrarily selected from a space-time continuum in which the process of change is occurring. Indeed the great danger of thinking about race in terms of statistical averages is that these become converted into racial standards representing static racial entities.[46] In reality no human or animal group is static and immutable. The phenomenon of race in particular is something plastic and dynamic.

Thus whatever reality attaches to race is extremely qualified and tenuous. As such it does not permit the adopting of practical attitudes towards individuals on the basis of their so-called racial characteristics. The consequences of this for the ethics of race relations should be evident.

Notes

1. Cf. Jacques Barzun, *Race: A Study in Modern Superstition* (London, 1938), Ch. VII.

2. Among the best known works of Quatrefages are his *Rapport sur le progrès de l'Anthropologie* (1867), *L'Espèce humaine* (1877), and *Histoire générale des races humaines* (1889).

3. Cf. also R. Martin, *Lehrbuch der Anthropologie* (1914).

4. Cf. L. C. Dunn and Th. Dobzhansky, *Heredity, Race and Society* (New York, 1957), p. 109. In the present chapter I am much indebted to this little classic on human differences.

5. Cf. Ashley Montague, *Man in Process* (New York, 1962), p. 106.

6. *Ibid.*, p. 107.

7. Blumenbach (1752–1840) was a professor in the Faculty of Medicine at Göttingen. The first to place anthropology on a really rational basis, in his *De generis humani varietate nativa* (1775–1795) he laid the foundations of race classification based on physical measurement.

8. Cf. H. Vallois, "Race," in *Anthropology Today* (Chicago, 1957), pp. 146–148.

9. Cited in Vallois, *op. cit.*, p. 146. In order of time, after Aristotle, Vesalius is the second greatest name in the history of anthropology.

10. Perhaps the most extreme exponent of this view was Sir William Laurence (1783–1867) who, in his *Lectures on Comparative Anatomy*, attributed the flat noses and thick lips of the Negro to the method of carrying babies in Africa. As the mothers carry their infants on their backs, he said, "in the violent motions required for their hard labor, as in beating or pounding millet, the face of the child is said to be constantly thumping against the back of the mother."

11. Cited in Vallois, *loc. cit.*

12. *Ibid.*

13. *Ibid.*

14. Cf. his article in *Bulletin de la Societé d'Anthropologie*, June, 1889; cf. also his *Les races et les peuples de la terre* (Paris, 1900).

15. *Rassenkunde und Rassengeshichte*, 2nd ed. (Stuttgart, 1938–1944).

16. C. S. Coon, S. M. Garn and J. B. Birdsell, *Races: A Study of the Problems of Race Formation in Man* (Springfield, Ill., 1950).

17. Cf. Dunn and Dobzhansky, *op. cit.*, pp. 118–121, and A. Richmond, *The Colour Problem* (London, 1961), p. 15.

18. Cf. Montague, *op. cit.*, p. 145.

19. Cf. Montague, *op. cit.*, p. 144.

20. Cf. Vallois, *op. cit.*, pp. 150–151, and Raymond Firth, *Human Types* (New York, 1958).

21. Cf. Haddon, *A History of Anthropology* (London, 1910), p. 34. Grattan's article appeared in the *Ulster Journal of Archaeology* in 1858. Grattan wrote: "No single cranium can *per se* be taken to represent the average characteristics of the variety from which it may be derived. It is only from a large deduction that the ethnologist can venture to pronounce with confidence upon the normal type of any race."

22. P. Topinard, *L'Anthropologie* (Paris, 1876).

23. *Op. cit.*, p. 23.

24. *The Origin of Races* (New York, 1962). Cf. also Coon, *The Living Races of Man* (London, 1966).

25. By J. S. Weiner, reader in physical anthropology at Oxford, in a review of Coon's book in *The Sunday Times* (London), May 19, 1965; also Nigel Barnicot, professor of physical anthropology, University College, London, in a review in the London *Observer*, May 26, 1965.

26. Cf. Weiner, *loc. cit.*

27. Cf. V. P. Yakimov, "Races and Time," at Unesco discussion on biological aspects of race, Moscow, 1964, published in *The International Social Science Journal*, XVII (1965), No. 1, 154.

28. Cf. H. Vallois, *op. cit.*, pp. 148–149.

29. Cf. Dunn and Dobzhansky, *op. cit.*, pp. 115–117.

30. Cf. Vallois, *op. cit.*, p. 155.

31. Cf. Firth, *op. cit.*, pp. 18–19.

32. Cf. Dunn and Dobzhansky, *op. cit.*, p. 127–128.

33. *Ibid.*, p. 126.

34. In *Anthropologie Générale*.

35. Cf. Vallois, *op. cit.*, pp. 155–156.

36. Cf. Franz Boas (1858–1942), *The Mind of Primitive Man* (New York, 1938); *Race, Language and Culture* (New York, 1940).

37. G. Pierre Paul Broca (1824–1880), "La race celtique ancienne et moderne" in *Revue d'Anthropologie*, I.

38. Tadeusz Bielicki, "Typologists versus populationists and genetic Theory" in *The International Social Science Journal*, XVII (1965), No. 1.

39. Cf. V. V. Bunak, "The study of population and local races" in *The International Social Science Journal, loc. cit.*

40. Richmond, *op. cit.*, p. 16.

41. In the case of the inhabitants of Clare Island off the Irish coast, for example, a study of their surnames convinced Professor Eoin MacNeill that half of them came originally from Norway, Scotland or Wales while many of the others were also of foreign ancestry. Similarly, Dr. Earle Hackett of Trinity College, Dublin, in a paper delivered some years ago entitled "Irish Blood Group Studies," estimated that some 70 percent of the Aran Islanders sprang from English seventeenth century ancestors. He added that blood grouping has provided evidence that most of the Irish nation sprang from one or more of the older peoples of Europe who long ago were pushed to the west by the pressure of growing populations in the north and east of the Continent. Just as it has been shown that modern Hungarian Gypsies of Hindu origin have the same blood group frequencies as modern Hindus in India, even though the Gypsies have lived in Hungary for hundreds of years, so too Irish blood groups have much in common with the peoples of England, Scotland and the Welsh Highlands, and possibly some now isolated peoples of Mediterranean shores, while in the eastern half of Ireland there is English blood which came in after the Anglo-Norman conquest. In the case of Aran, maintained Dr. Hackett, there is historical evidence that a succession of English military forces was stationed in the island for about one hundred years around the seventeenth century and no record has yet been found of the last garrison having been withdrawn. This numerical infusion, plus the introduction of the potato simultaneously, would have allowed the mixed Irish and English stock to become an expanded population—the ancestors of the present-day islanders. Cf. E. MacNeill, *Early Irish Laws and Institutions* (Dublin, 1934).

42. Cf. Firth, *op. cit.*, pp. 20–22.

43. Published in *The International Social Science Journal*, XVII (1965), No. 1.

44. R. A. Fisher, *The Genetical Theory of Natural Selection* (Oxford, 1930), p. 174.

45. Cf. Montague, *op. cit.*, pp. 91–92.

46. *Ibid.*, p. 109.

For Further Reading

E. J. Alpenfels, *Sense and Nonsense about Race*, New York, 1946.

Th. Dobzhansky, *Mankind Evolving*, New Haven, 1962.

Otto Clineberg, *Race and Society*, Paris, 1952.

C. S. Coon, *The Races of Europe*, New York, 1939.

C. S. Coon, S. M. Garn and J. B. Birdsell, *Races: A Study of the Problem of Race Formation in Man*, Springfield, Ill., 1950.

Christine Doyle, "The Great Caucasoid Myth," in *The Observer*, 31 March, 1968.

A. L. Kroeber, *Anthropology Today: An Encyclopedic Inventory*, Chicago, 1953.

H. Lundborg and F. J. Linders, *Racial Characters of the Swedish Nation*, Stockholm, 1926.

C. McWilliams, *Brothers under the Skin*, Boston, 1943.

Ashley Montague, *The Concept of Race*, New York, 1964.

———, "A Cursory Examination of the Relations between Physical and Social Anthropology" in *American Journal of Physical Anthropology*, XXVI (1940), 41–61.

———, *An Introduction to Physical Anthropology*, 3rd edition, Springfield, Ill., 1960.

———, *Man's Most Dangerous Myth*, New York, 1945.

M. Nesturkh, *The Races of Mankind*, Moscow (Foreign Languages Publishing House), 1965.

H. J. Seligmann, *Race against Man*, New York, 1939.

"Who are the British?" I—The Conquerors, in *The Observer*, 12 February, 1967; II—The Immigrants, in *The Observer*, 19 February, 1967.

CHAPTER III

Race Theories: European and American

Despite the fact that the essential unity of the human race has long been defended by anthropologists, theories concerning the biological purity and natural superiority of some races continue to be held by many. Such theories and their immediate correlatives concerning the existence of inferior races involve important practical consequences. It follows naturally from these theories that the superior races should be allowed freedom of expansion while inferior races should yield place to them where necessary.

European Race Theories

Racism, as this attitude is most commonly termed, is associated particularly in modern times with the theory of the superiority of the Nordic race, centered in the German people. This theory was first proposed in 1853 by the Frenchman, Count Joseph de Gobineau (1816–1862), who held that among Europeans the superior people is that of the Aryan Germans of northern France and Belgium.[1] Gobineau's theory emerged as part of an explanation of the reasons for the fall of civilizations, which, according to Gobineau, has always been due to a deterioration through crossbreeding of the racial quality of their original stocks. Hence the importance of keeping racial strains as pure as possible.

For Gobineau there were three great races, the White, the Black and the Yellow. Of these the White race only is really balanced and capable of founding a culture. Gobineau maintained that there are three branches to the White race—the

49

Hamites, the Semites and the Aryans. Of the three, the latter, who have their finest flowering in the Germanic peoples, are by far the most highly gifted. They should be afforded every effort to develop and expand.

This theory was further developed by the Englishman, Houston Chamberlain (1855–1926), who surpassed Gobineau in his belief in the superiority of the Aryan stock. He included in it the Celtic, Teutonic and Slavonic peoples, in other words, the northern European peoples in general. "Physically and mentally," he wrote, "the Aryans surpass all other men; therefore they are by right (as Aristotle says) the masters of the world."[2]

Chamberlain was here referring to the *locus classicus* of the idea that some men are superior to others while, at the opposite extreme, some are somewhat less than human. In the third chapter of the *Politics* Aristotle had propounded the view that "a complete family is formed of persons and slaves" and that "it cannot be doubted that there are some men born for liberty as others are for slavery." It was this passage that Chamberlain used for the purpose of glorifying the Aryan peoples. In addition he did this in a markedly anti-Semitic way that had not at all been associated with Gobineau. This constituted the starting-point of the belief in the superiority of the Teutonic race with its consequent and related anti-Semitism.

The theory was further developed under the Hitler régime by Alfred Rosenberg, who was responsible for the implementation of practical measures to restore the purity, and ensure the spread, of the Teutonic peoples.[3] Everything came to be subordinated to the over-riding importance of race. "All true culture," said Rosenberg, "is the conscious form taken by the growing life force of a race." And again, "Right is what is advantageous to the Volk."

Although racism has come to be linked particularly with the Gobineau-Chamberlain-Rosenberg tradition, it should not be forgotten that it has had many historical counterparts. It was to be found earlier in Greek, Roman and Celtic ideas of superiority, corresponding French ideas after the Revolution and under Napoleon, and British beliefs during the days of Victorian imperialism.

There are, however, British racist elements of more ancient lineage. During the 1640's, for example, the New England settlers passed three resolutions to the effect that the earth is the property of the Lord, that the Lord has given the earth to his chosen people and that they—the settlers themselves—were his chosen ones.[4] Daniel Defoe, in his book *The True Born English-man*, published in 1701, ridiculed the racial arrogance of the English people and in particular their belief in the inferiority of the Celt to the Anglo-Saxon.[5]

But the high point of British racism was reached under Victoria. It was Cecil Rhodes who asked: "Have you ever thought how lucky you are to be born an Englishman when there are so many millions who were not?" In 1903, in his famous Will, Rhodes gave utterance to the then common belief of Englishmen that Britain, the British dominions, Germany and the United States of America, being peopled by Teutonic stock, were naturally superior to southern European, Celtic and other countries, and that they should form a sort of oligarchy which would dominate the world—all of which caused one British writer to exclaim: "We condemned as false and dangerous the racialism which was promulgated thirty years later by Hitler. But we carry a considerable moral responsibility for having helped to disseminate these ideas."[6]

British racism has been as persistent and recurring as it has been unwilling to show its true colors openly. Nevertheless, at the Peace Conference in 1919, Lord Balfour revealed a racist attitude of mind by declaring that "If it was true that in one sense all the members of any given nation had been created equal, it was not true that a Central African was the equal of the European."[7]

Such racists frequently regard colonial peoples as having been the recipients of a sort of external grace through contact with their British overlords. It was in this context that Mr. Tariq Ali, Pakistani president of the Oxford Union, speaking in 1965 against race prejudice in England, said that there appeared to be less discrimination against Asian than African Students. "I suppose Indians and Pakistanis," he said, "vaguely remind these kind of people of Maharajahs and polo and all that."[8]

Race Theories in the United States

Nor has America been free of racist ideas. In the United States they received a considerable fillip in the nineteenth century by reason of the influence of Darwinian thinking.[9] The sub-title to Darwin's *The Origin of Species* (1859) was "The Preservation of Favored Races in the Struggle for Life," and in his *The Descent of Man* (1871), he had written that it was likely that the backward races would disappear before the advance of higher civilizations. Such views could not but conduce to the encouragement of racism. Not that Darwinism was the only cause of racist thinking. Neither in Europe, influenced by *Machtpolitik* ideas, nor in England, where modern nationalism and the romantic movement had earlier given rise to Anglo-Saxonism, nor in the United States, where slavery had already existed for some time, were Darwinian ideas exclusively responsible for furthering racist tendencies. Nevertheless they played an important part.

Prominent among American thinkers on the subject was the sociologist William Graham Sumner (1840–1910), for whom the progress of civilization depended upon the process of natural selection. Despite the fact that it negated the traditional American ideology of equality and natural rights, his basic principle of social evolution was the survival of the fittest. "There can be no rights against Nature," he said, "except to get out of her whatever we can, which is only the fact of the struggle for existence."[10] Against this background it is understandable that he should have held that every social system has its inevitable evils, among which poverty and racial conflict are outstanding examples.

Lester Ward (1841–1913) was another distinguished American who thought along similar lines, although he cannot be classed among the Social Darwinists. The bases of his social system were radically different from those of Darwin and Herbert Spencer. His views bore a marked similarity to theirs, however, because of the influence on him of the European "conflict school" of Ludwig Gumplowicz (1838–1909), for which war, conquest and racial conflict were necessary preconditions of human progress.

It is only natural that ideas such as these, put forward by eminent men of letters, should eventually come to be offered in more popular form and gradually affect men's attitudes and behavior. By 1885 they had gained firm root.[11] In that year John Fiske, in a lecture entitled "Manifest Destiny," recommended a militant imperialism for America, and the Reverend Josiah Strong, in his book *Our Country: Its Possible Future and Its Present Crisis*, maintained that a new and better physical type was emerging in the United States. He believed that the unoccupied lands of the world were filling up and that there would be a competition of races and a struggle for survival.

In a somewhat similar vein, Theodore Roosevelt in 1899 produced a book entitled *The Strenuous Life*, and another in 1910 called *The New Nationalism*. Another American, Albert T. Beveridge, carried the matter to its logical conclusion, maintaining that the English and Teutonic peoples were in the design of God "the master organizers of the world."

In this climate of opinion it would be a brave man indeed who would venture to express a note of dissent. Some there were who were prepared to do so, for example the pragmatists, who believed in the efficacy of ideas rather than of conflict for social reform, and people like William Ripley, who, in 1897, sought through his book, *The Races of Europe*, to discredit the Aryan myth before the American public.

By and large, however, these dissenters had but little influence and racist thinking came to have an ever-increasing practical import. To a considerable degree it may be said to have been responsible for the Anglo-American alliance of the end of the century. Indeed its effects began to be felt on an ever-broader front. In 1904 Jack London warned of a threat to the Anglo-Saxon world from the Japanese, while Hugh Lusk insisted that this was only part of a more general threat from the yellow peoples. At this time talk of the "Yellow Peril" reached its height and it is not without significance that the years in question, just prior to and immediately after World War I, were precisely those that saw the publication in America of Madison Grant's *The Passing of The Great Race* (1916), and Lothrop Stoddard's *The Rising Tide of Color* (1920) and *Racial Realities in Europe* (1925).

Superiority or Inferiority?

No less than continental European, British and American ideas of superiority have automatically entailed a belief in the inferiority of other races. Delving back into history,[12] we find the sixteenth-century English traveler William Cunningham writing that the Indians were "comparable to brute beasts."[13] In 1707 the Quaker John Archdale could see the hand of God in operation "in killing the Indians to make room for the English," and in 1714 John Lawson wrote of the Caroline Indians: "We look upon them with scorn and disdain and think them little better than beasts in human shape." We read too that "when Dr. Wardell of Sydney defended an Englishman charged with the murder of a Black, he argued from Lord Bacon, Puffendorf, and Barbeyrac, that savages who fed upon human flesh (as the Australians were by him assumed to do) were proscribed by the law of nature; consequently it was no offense to slay them." And in 1796 a paper to the Manchester Philosophical Society, entitled "An Account of the Regular Gradations in Man," argued that the Negro was "nearer to the brute creation than to any other human species."

American racism issued in an analogous pejorative attitude towards non-white races, particularly the Negro. In the early nineteenth century the anthropologist Glidden wrote: "There is no such thing as a common human nature . . . White men and red men, yellow men and black men, have no more original relationship to each other than the bears of Nepal to the tigers of Africa. . . . Their organization dooms them to slavery. . . ."[14] For Glidden and his like the Negro "was no real human being but a domestic animal."

To the mid-nineteenth-century American, therefore, A. H. Stevens' famous "Corner-Stone" speech at Savannah on March 21, 1861 was no surprise. "It is a mistake," said Stevens, "to assert that all races are equal. Our government [i.e. that of the Confederate States] is based on diametrically opposed ideas. The corner-stone of its foundation is a great truth: the Black is not the equal of the White; servitude, subordination to the White race is his natural moral position. Our government is the first in the history of the world to be based on this great physical, philosophical and moral truth."[15] In 1863 the chief justice of the United States Supreme Court confirmed this value judgment, declaring that it was an axiom that could not be disputed.[16]

Today one can find very similar ideas about racial superiority and inferiority being tossed about in the context of the American color problem. They are not at all confined to any one side. If on the one extreme one comes upon them in the utterances of the American Nazi Party of George Lincoln Rockwell, with its battle cry of "White Power," on the other extreme they are equally to be found in the new philosophy of "Black Power," which rejects the white man and all integration with him.

And as whites are to be found for and against white racist ideas, so also there are Negroes for and against black ones. It is heartening to read that at the 1966 annual convention of the

National Association for the Advancement of Colored People (NAACP) held in Los Angeles, Vice President Hubert Humphrey was roundly applauded when he declared: "Racism is racism— and there is no room in America for racism of any color."[17]

These sentiments need much repeating, both inside and outside the U.S.A.[18]

Notes

1. Cf. J. de Gobineau, *Essai sur l'Inégalité des Races Humaines* (Paris, 1853).

2. H. Chamberlain, *Foundations of the Nineteenth Century* (London, 1899).

3. A. Rosenberg, *Der Myth des 20 Jahrhunderts* (Munich, 1930).

4. Cf. L. Hanke, *Aristotle and the American Indians* (London, 1959).

5. Cf. also J. M. Robertson, *The Saxon and the Celt* (London, 1897).

6. Colin Clark, *Australia's Hopes and Fears* (London, 1958), p. 45.

7. Cited in Robert Delavignette, *Christianity and Colonialism* (London, 1964), p. 93.

8. As reported in *The Sunday Times* (London), April 11, 1965.

9. Cf. Richard Hofstadter, *Social Darwinism in American Thought* (Boston, 1955). Cf. also Hertz, *op. cit.*, pp. 12–13.

10. In *What Social Classes Owe to Each Other* (New York, 1883), p. 73.

11. Cf. Hofstadter, *op. cit.*, p. 178 seq.

12. Cf. Hanke, *op. cit.*, pp. 100–101.

13. *The Cosmographical Glasse* (London, 1559).

14. Cited in Hanke, *op. cit.*, p. 102.

15. Cited in Delavignette, *op. cit.*, pp. 92–93.

16. *Ibid.*

17. Quoted in *The New York Times* (International Edition), July 11, 1966.

18. It should be noted that the predominantly Anglo-Saxon racist ideas that have been characteristic of America have been opposed sporadically by others of Celtic inspiration. Thus in the years immediately after the Civil War the Anglo-Saxon myth drew a re- action in the shape of a Celtic interpretation of history. Prominent

among the later ideological supports of this movement was the book by the Irish priest, Father Ulick Bourke, entitled *The Aryan Origins of the Gaelic Race and Language* (1876), which got an enthusiastic reception in Boston. There was also the writing of the eccentric Martin O'Brennan, who maintained that the language of the Celts had been the speech of the Garden of Eden (See his contribution to the American publication *Irish World*, 23 February, 1878, and *Ancient Ireland*, Dublin, 1855). Leaning on these and other supports, such as Matthew Arnold's *Study of Celtic Literature*, a series of American Philo-Celtic societies sought to spread the idea that it was a peculiarly Celtic genius to fuse together disparate racial groups and to give birth to democratic institutions, or as one writer has put it, "to insist that the foundations of America rested on the Blarney stone, not on Plymouth Rock" (Cf. Thomas N. Brown, "The Origins and Character of Irish-American Nationalism", *The Review of Politics*, vol. 18 (1956), n 3, pp. 342–343).

For Further Reading

H. Coudenhove-Kalergi, *Anti-Semitism throughout the Ages*, London, 1935.

J. Finot, *Le prejugé des races*, Paris, 1906.

F. H. Hankins, *Racial Basis of Civilization*, New York, 1926.

G. Montandon, *La race, les races*, Paris, 1933.

E. Pittard, *Race and History*, New York, 1926.

T. Simar, *Etude critique sur la formation de la doctrine des races*, Brussels, 1922.

CHAPTER IV

Race Prejudice: Britain Today

Race prejudice is one of three items that are usually covered by the general description "The Color Bar." The other two are racial discrimination and racial segregation, which will be treated in separate chapters.

Race prejudice is a subjective attitude of mind towards people, usually, though not exclusively, by reason of the pigmentation of their skin. It is frequently associated with a tendency to exaggerate the differences between the parties concerned.

Race prejudice is a rather complicated phenomenon. In common with prejudice in general, it may be said to involve three basic elements. First of all, it is founded on a mistaken judgment, itself due to the processes of hearsay and generalization. Secondly, it embraces a deviant will attitude, that is, at least some admixture of ill will. And thirdly, it includes some concomitant emotional complexes. In common with anti-Semitism, xenophobia, and religious fanaticism, race prejudice can be either negative, that is, mild in nature, or positive, that is, violent. Like them, too, it can be either a personal or a group phenomenon.

Whether this attitude will remain latent or express itself overtly depends largely on the amount of contact between the parties involved and their relative strength and social status. As an experienced writer on the subject has said: "The problem arises when individual prejudices become widespread and the people holding them support one another in their attitude."[1]

When this happens racial conflict is almost certain to erupt and the road is open to racial discrimination. It is the uncontrolled evolution of such a situation that is most to be feared in situations of racial tension. For the product of thousands of little irritants can add up to a mighty explosion. And as has been wisely pointed out by a student of race conflict, "when two races are not consciously preparing themselves to live democratically, frictions occur in over-crowded street cars, parks, swimming pools, motion picture houses, restaurants and the like."[2]

The Causes of Race Prejudice

Physical. The causes of race prejudice merit examination.[3] The earliest effort at an explanation of its origins is probably the "instinct theory" of the philosopher John Dewey. According to Dewey, prejudice in general is an instinctive dislike of what is strange, in the case of race prejudice, in response to physical differences. This theory fell into disrepute when experiments with young children showed no traces of such dislike. It was followed by the "behaviorist theory" of John B. Watson.[4] For the behaviorists, race prejudice is a product of conditioned reflexes, strange features and the like becoming associated with responses to unfavorable stimuli. However, this too was gradually abandoned as it came to be realized that it did not cover all types of race prejudice.

Economic. For some time now, in certain quarters, the causes of race prejudice have been elaborated in terms of Marxist theory.[5] In accordance with its concept of social processes in general, this theory maintains that race prejudice is a mechanism by which the dominant group in society stigmatizes other groups as inferior so that they can be kept down. Shorn of its specifically Marxist aspects and intentions, the valid and worthwhile residual element in this explanation has been used by Gunnar Myrdal to develop his "interest theory."[6] For Myrdal and his followers race prejudice is something which tends to serve the interests of the majority group in society. Defenders of the "interest theory" are persuaded that each of the "beliefs" connected with any particular form of race prejudice is tailored to dovetail into an appropriate form of discrimination. For example, the belief that Negroes get sleepy at machines is admirably suited to cause discrimination against them in the matter of jobs.

One does not have to be a Marxist to see that social stratification is determined largely by the economic system and that therefore economic interests can play a powerful part in evoking prejudice, including racial prejudice, against any group whose presence or growth in a given society is likely to upset that society's ideal economic equilibrium. Thus along the Pacific coast of the United States, where Chinese and Japanese immigrants constitute an appreciable economic threat, there is a considerable degree of prejudice against them, whereas along the U.S. Atlantic coast, where they are much fewer in number, this is not so. The same phenomenon has been observed in England during the past few years as the inflow of West Indian workers has increased.

Of the "interest theory" explanation, however, it should be observed that, while it is true in so far as it goes, it is important to qualify it. Interest factors are themselves dependent on cultural factors for the direction taken by individual and group aggressiveness. There is no necessary correlation between difficult economic circumstances and the presence of race prejudice; theoretically at least, it should be possible to find excellent race relations side by side with the existence of quite serious economic difficulties.

Sociological. For suchlike reasons, contemporary students of race prejudice tend to gravitate towards broader sociological and psychological elements of explanation. According to the "sociological theory" of William Graham Sumner[7] and Franklin Henry

Giddings,[8] race prejudice results from social processes created by the force of "consciousness of kind," which tends towards the formation of like-minded groups. For the "psychological theory," on the other hand, race prejudice is a sort of rationalization, through aggressive attitudes towards others, of one's own feelings of guilt or insecurity. This effort at explanation—sometimes called "the scapegoat theory"—is used to explain the reasons for the venting of spleen on bosses, labor and political leaders, and religious as well as racial groups.

Psychological. This approach is further developed by the depth psychologists. For the Freudians race prejudice in general is a sign of sex frustration of some kind on the part of a group. There may well be some truth in this idea. The reader of James Baldwin's autobiographical books[9] cannot fail to notice the rather strong sexual overtones to the author's discussion of some aspects of the race question. And the writer of a chapter on "Sex and Settlers" in Africa has the following to say on the matter:

> The television programs about Rhodesia scrupulously avoid the sex issue. The normal run of press comment does not touch on it. Yet the psychiatrists and race-relations experts who have studied the black-white problem in Africa are in no doubt that deep sexual guilt feelings, stemming from the rapine of pioneer days and the fear of future African revenge, are vital to an understanding of the white man's behavior where he is still in control of society. It may even be that this unrecognized, unmentioned sexual complex is the central driving force behind all the outward political actions of Rhodesia's white settlers. . . . Unfortunately for race relations in the Rhodesias, events in the Congo have reinforced the deep-buried sexual apprehensions of the settler minority holding power in Salisbury.[10]

The reference here is to the effect of the sensational press accounts of the raping of white women in the chaos of the Belgian departure.

For Alfred Adler's camp, on the other hand, the inadequacies attributed to another racial group are used by the group which partakes of the prejudice for the purpose of covering up its own defects, which more often than not are imaginary rather than real and stem from inferiority complexes of one kind or another. With or without complexes, there is in any case a deep-seated tendency in people to blame their troubles, however wrongly, on causes outside themselves.

Finally, there is a Jungian version of the nature and causes of race prejudice. According to this theory, all such prejudice is really an atavistic fear of racial intermarriage, a fear which stems from an irrational horror of cross-breeding, viewed as the rape of the female carrier of the racial inheritance:

> Every other justification for the color bar can be annihilated by logic, but not this, for its emotional potential is such that the nerve of many Europeans who are on the point of abandoning their discriminatory attitudes fails them when the abhorrent prospect is described in concrete terms. It is this fear which the segregationist exploits to provide the last and most effective shot in his locker. When he is really cornered . . . he can blast his way out with the most overworked projectile in the racial battle: The Question. "Would you like your daughter to marry an African?" Immediately all kinds of unspoken fears are exposed. The revulsion . . . confounds logic. Those who can be persuaded to talk about it think in terms of white purity being ravaged by black savagery. Possibly the violence of the reaction stems from some atavistic dread deep in the primitive psychology of the race . . . a tribal instinct for protecting the female as the bearer of the race's posterity.[11]

It is more than likely that each of these theories contains some elements of an adequate explanation of the causes of race prejudice. One-sided explanations of anything are usually insufficient. One American sociologist seems to put the matter well when he says that "a well rounded theory of the genesis of prejudice would include many of these single-factor theories . . .

[and] it would take into account the demonstrated fact that prejudice is learned, not inherited, and that the learning of wholesome attitudes in place of prejudicial ones would solve many of the problems arising from socially undesirable prejudices."[12]

How Can Race Prejudice be Eradicated?

For the eradication of race prejudice some sociologists, such as R. A. Schermerhorn,[13] believe above all in the possibilities of an adequate educational program. As they see things, such an approach is far more effective than a head-on attack. They insist that the elimination of discriminatory institutions associated with race prejudice is never in itself an adequate solution. It is the mentality which gives rise to them that needs changing.

Others, such as Robert MacIver,[14] place very great store on an attack on the discriminatory institutions that usually go with race prejudice. It is easier and more practicable they say, than to try to change attitudes or feelings directly. Indeed the one sure way to modify these feelings is to eliminate the institutional bases which support them. This, however, is far from certain. At least theoretically, it would seem to be quite possible to find race prejudice even in a non-discriminatory and non-segregated society. It must also be remembered that prejudice is something learned, not inherited, and is therefore subject to the influence of education.

These considerations make clear the importance of a sound education and formation in matters concerning race. As one anthropologist has put it, the kind of education for the elimination of race prejudice is "education for humanity first and in the facts afterward. For what use are facts unless they are intelligently understood and humanly used?"[15] This is especially true in the case of race prejudice, which is to a large extent a moral problem. In the United States, for example, a study by the Industrial Relations Counsellors concluded that "among a significant number of companies a motivating factor for employment of Negroes was the personal philosophy held by some individual or group in the management that it was the right thing to do."[16] And an American Jesuit, emphasizing the point that the race question in the United States is neither a sociological nor a legal problem exclusively, but also a moral problem, has written: "Racism, whether by the compulsion of unconstitutional statutes in the South or by the force of un-Christian snobbery in the North, is essentially the same vicious evil. It is fundamentally a moral evil. It cannot be completely eliminated by the courts of law; it must be eradicated from the hearts of men."[17]

From the educational point of view, the following type of psychological explanation of the nature and causes of race prejudice represents one of the most valuable approaches to the problem:

> Prejudicial attitudes are a means of resolving inner conflicts and of handling anxieties the origins of which are largely unconscious. . . . It is highly significant that investigations of the psychological origins of prejudice have shown that the people most inclined to be intolerant are those who feel insecure and are afraid of losing their present social status. Insecurity often leads to aggressiveness and this may be directed towards some socially acceptable target such as is provided in a heterogeneous society by the existence of other cultural or racial groups. Once created, unfavorable attitudes towards other ethnic groups tend to be rationalized and justified. The coercion of subordinates by discrimination and other means provides, in many societies, a socially accepted outlet for aggressive impulses.[18]

Race Relations in British History

Because of the present actuality of the race question in Britain it may be of interest to take a bird's eye conspectus of British attitudes towards race during the course of history. The matter first arose in connection with the practice of slavery. In this matter, as in so many others, the British attitude was determined primarily by what were later known as the principles of mercantilism. If the British would not own slaves themselves, they were not to be inhibited from selling them to others. The first ship to sail from Britain carrying slaves for Spaniards in the West Indies was that of Sir John Hawkins in 1562. From then on for over a century some 20,000 slaves were transported to the New World every year in British ships with few voices raised in protest. But it was the eighteenth century that saw the greatest expansion of the English slave trade. For example, the number of Liverpool slave-ships increased from one in 1709 to fifteen in 1726 and a hundred in 1770, when at least a quarter of Liverpool ships were slavers.

In itself, of course, the slave trade did not necessarily imply the existence of race theories or race prejudice in Britain. Indeed the business seems to have been fundamentally economic in motivation. "The reasons for slavery," said Edward Gibbon Wakefield during the period when it flourished, "are not moral but economic circumstances; they relate not to vice and virtue, but to production." In her Reith Lectures on the subject of colonialism, Marjorie Perham has been rather devastating about the role which political aggrandizement and economic self-interest have played in advancing the expansion of the British Empire and colonies.[19] Up to the third quarter of the eighteenth century, she says, the purposes of the empire were mainly those of economic growth (expansion of trade) and national security (the protection of commerce). Towards the end of the century these came under attack from the humanitarians, who were against colonialism because of its implications in the matter of the slave trade. During the nineteenth century, however, the challenge of the philanthropists was evaded on the plea that the colonies were necessary for the purpose of emigration. In reality, of course, under the aegis of this, it was a quest for power and prestige that was the main object of nineteenth-century British colonialism.

The role of the slave trade in the earlier colonial period is interesting to us here because it had definite implications for contemporary British attitudes to race. Early writers were disposed to defend the trade in the name of morality. As is usual in the case of books of that period, the titles serve as a full guide to the contents. Thus, in 1772, the Reverend Thomas Thompson submitted a tract entitled *The Trade in Negro Slaves on the African Coast in Accordance with Human Principles and the Laws of Revealed Religion*. As late as 1852, the Reverend Josiah Preit published *A Bible Defence of Slavery*, and there were many similar books and pamphlets.

But these views were far from reigning uncontested. The Quakers were opposed to the slave trade from the beginning. In 1783 the prime minister, Lord Frederick North, complimented them for their humanity but regretted that the abolition of the slave trade was nevertheless impossible because it had become necessary to almost every nation in Europe.[20] They were supported, however, by John Wesley and the evangelical movements, which maintained that slaves, no less than white people, were children of God. Gradually an anti-slavery movement got under way, drawing strength from a variety of sources. As Miss Perham has put it, to the Christians—first the Quakers and then the Evangelicals—it was sin; to the new romantic movement it was ugly; to the emerging radical philosophers it was unnatural, and to the rising liberal economists it was uneconomic.[21]

The convergence of these streams provided a powerful impetus for the eventual abolition of the slave trade. It has been estimated, however, that the religious impulse provided the strongest and most constant pressure to that end.[22] At any rate the slave trade was abolished in 1807 and the institution of slavery itself in 1833. But while humanitarian and religious considerations played an important part in achieving this, it was also helped by economic considerations, in particular an attack by capitalist manu-facturers in Britain against the general West Indian trade monopoly, whose preferential sugar duties particularly irritated them.

Some connection between the slave trade or slavery on the one hand and race prejudice or racism on the other would scarcely have been possible to avoid. During the period of the slave trade and even after it certain racist attitudes were subscribed to by the British. This emerges, for example, from the *Report of the Select Committee on Aborigines*, which was published by The Aborigines Protection Movement in 1837, and which criticized prevailing attitudes to subject peoples. "The British Empire," said this document, "has been signally blessed by Providence in her eminence, her strength, her wealth, her prosperity . . . These were given for some higher purpose than commercial prosperity and military renown . . . He who has made Great Britain what she is will require at our hands how we have employed the influence He has lent to us in our dealings with the untutored and defenseless savages." And it was Mark Twain who wrote: "Whether Cecil Rhodes is the lofty patriot multitudes believe him to be, or Satan come again, when he stands at the Cape his shadow falls to the Zambesi. He robs and slays, and enslaves the Matabele, and gets Charter-Christian applause for it."[23]

It is not without significance for an understanding of the racist aspect of slavery that the Anti-Slavery and Aborigines Protection Societies should have combined forces in 1909. Since that date they have combated all forms of racism in the colonies, gathering information on abuses all over the empire and elsewhere and leading deputations to the colonial foreign secretary demanding reform. Recently in Britain itself they have been joined by CARD—the Campaign Against Racial Discrimination—which got under way following the visit to Britain at the end of 1964 of the American Negro leader, Dr. Martin Luther King.[24] For in Britain today, as in the days of the slave trade, a number of questions relating to race overlap. This is particularly true of race prejudice and opposition to colored immigration.

That race prejudice in Britain is to some extent connected with the colored problem first became evident from a series of articles entitled "The Dark Million" which *The Times* of London carried during January, 1965. It is likely at least that the extent of this prejudice is something new and that it has grown concurrently with the number of colored people in Britain. Between 1955 and 1958, before these numbers really became striking, the author of an otherwise excellent book on West Indian workers in London could dismiss the color element as irrelevant to the problem of prejudice against those people.[25] As she saw it then, the problem was essentially that of immigration, not of color, and, as in the case of the Jews and the Irish, the odds might be said to lie heavily in favor of the likelihood of West Indian assimilation within two or three generations.

That things have changed since 1958 cannot be doubted and there is certainly color prejudice in Britain today. Such prejudice is bound to be connected with the publicity given to estimates such as that between 170,000 and 300,000 colored children or half-castes have been already born in Britain and that by the year 2000 the colored population of Britain will be in the region of 3,000,000. It also affects attitudes to colored people in the labor market, as a London newspaper reported:

Jobs are sometimes denied them because of the hostility of white workers. Firms are reluctant to talk about it. One personnel manager in a West London firm employing colored workers admitted eventually: "Twice we have reduced or stopped taking colored people on, temporarily, in order to maintain a balance, say of twenty percent or thirty percent colored. If you get to forty percent colored in a factory you are in a position wherein you cannot possibly stop it becoming a permanently colored factory. Officially there is no color bar in the unions. But you get pressure from the shop floor. They have sent their trade union officials and said that there were far too many here. Then they do a bargain— the same as with wages. They say, get the proportion of colored to ten percent, but really expect to get twenty percent. If you took on colored, and white people were unemployed, you would get pressure building up. We would want to employ white people anyway. They are much easier."[26]

The Race Relations Act, 1965

This is the background without which it is impossible to understand the British government's introduction of the 1965 Race Relations Act. It was passed on November 8 and came into operation one month later. That one of the primary purposes of this piece of legislation was the curbing of race prejudice should be evident to anybody who has followed government statements and debates on it. Thus in December, 1964, Prime Minister Harold Wilson declared that the government had ranged itself clearly against racial incitement, racial discrimination and the evil exploitation of racialism which still went on in Britain. "In your name," he told the Labor Conference, "I have condemned and will condemn every so-called Labor Club which operates color discrimination, every group of misguided workers who try to operate color prejudice in their working relations."[27]

The Act itself made clear the extent to which it was an instrument intended for the prevention of race prejudice. Section 1 of the Act made it unlawful for those in charge of hotels, public transport vehicles and other places of public resort to practice racial discrimination against persons seeking to use them. The Act established a race relations board and local conciliation committees to secure compliance with the section and resolve difficulties. This indicates that the approach of the Act was preventative rather than punitive.

In the last resort civil proceedings might be brought by the attorney general for its enforcement. Section 6 made it an offense for a person to disseminate written matter or, in a public place or at a public meeting, to use speech which is threatening, abusive or insulting or which is intended to stir up hatred against any section of the public in Great Britain distinguished by color, race, or by ethnic or national origins.

Some criticism was urged against the measure, at bill stage, on grounds of inadequacy. For example, Maurice Orbach, Labor member of Parliament for Stockport South, forwarded a survey of anti-Semitism in Britain to the home secretary requesting it to be considered as part of the background to the Race Relations Bill. Anti-Semitism, he argued, should be specifically prohibited by it.[28] This was in December, 1964. In February, 1965, an amendment to the bill was introduced to bring religious discrimination under the measure's provisions, that is, to make it illegal to stir up hatred against any religious section. This amendment was aimed especially at conditions in Northern Ireland. After discussion in the House, however, it was withdrawn.

CARD has continuously criticized the measure on this and other scores.[29] Although welcoming it as "an important expression of public policy," the group went on to say that it did not deal with the main problems facing colored people in Britain: "While the Bill prohibits discrimination in places in which it does not often occur (for example, ships, aircraft, theaters and cinemas), it fails to tackle the real problems in employment, local authority and private housing, advertising, insurance and the grant of credit facilities." Other loopholes, the statement went on to point out, are racial restrictions on the sale and resale of freehold properties, and discrimination on grounds of religion, which allows people to refuse to serve, say, Hindus, Muslims or Jews.

Of course it would be very difficult to frame successful legislation which would do all these things. One is reminded of the effort made by the League of Nations after its foundation to provide an adequate solution to the minorities problem which troubled Europe.[30] In his early drafts of the Articles of the Covenant of the League, President Woodrow Wilson included specific provisions relating to racial and national minorities. A separate clause for this purpose was inserted. "The League of Nations," it ran, "shall require all new states to bind themselves as a condition precedent to their recognition as independent or

autonomous states to accord to all racial or national minorities
within their several jurisdictions exactly the same treatment and
security both in law and in fact that is accorded to the racial or
national majority of their people." Very quickly, however, the
president's advisers commented that while the purpose of the
article was beneficent, general treatment on lines so broad was
impossible. The result was that in a new draft of the Covenant, of
February, 1920, the clause took on an entirely new shape. This,
as Hunter Miller has described it, was to the effect that members
of the League "will make no law prohibiting or interfering with
the free exercise of religion and that they will in no way discriminate either in law or in fact against those who practice any
particular creed, religion, or belief whose practices are not
inconsistent with public order or public morals."[31]

In this new draft legal protection against discrimination in
matters of religion entirely overshadowed protection against
racial discrimination. It was thought, perhaps, that by reason of
the connection between them, catering for the former was
sufficient to cover the latter as well. But it quickly became evident
that in the case of those countries whose entire populations
possessed the same religion but contained racial, linguistic or
other minorities, the clause would not fulfill the purpose for
which it was intended. The end of the matter was that, after
much debate, amendment and counter-amendment, the clause
was dropped entirely from the Covenant. States in whose cases
a minorities problem was thought likely to constitute particular
difficulty were required to give security for the proper treatment
of their minorities—particularly in the matter of religious liberty
—by way of special treaties either with the Allied Powers or the
League of Nations.

These difficulties encountered by the League in the way of
providing an all-embracing measure of anti-discrimination should
be remembered by critics of the 1965 British piece of legislation. It is well-nigh impossible to cover everything with one

blow. For this reason the positive criticism of the Society of Labor Lawyers is more helpful. Underlining the fact that the main value of the measure lay in its educational effect, the Society has suggested that the missing areas of discrimination, such as employment, can most successfully be tackled by means outside the criminal law. The best device for this, said its committee, is a conciliation commission, similar to bodies in the United States and Canada, where the majority of legitimate complaints are settled voluntarily without formal hearings or the application of sanctions.[32]

But in so far as legislation by way of its educational effect can help to eradicate race prejudice, it is obviously something beneficial and welcome. That race prejudice can be successfully overcome has been clearly proved by the Nottingham Survey "West Indians at Work."[33] The peculiar value of this survey has been to show that, although there were some problems concerning promotion and overtime, generally good relations at work existed between the West Indians and their white colleagues, relations markedly different from those connected with housing and social life. The lesson to be learned is that the possibility of better acquaintance through work can do much to remove the bases of race prejudice. It implies, too, that employers, whether voluntarily or with some stimulation, should do what they can to promote greater mixing in their work places. This is something which Britain's 1968 legislation can help to promote.

Notes

1. A. H. Richmond, *The Colour Problem* (London, 1955), pp. 19–20.
2. A. McClung Lee and N. D. Humphrey, *Race Riot* (New York, 1943), p. 6.
3. Cf. Albert T. Foley, S.J., "Minorities in American Society," in *Social Orientations* (St. Louis, 1956), p. 621.

4. Cf. J. B. Watson, *Behaviorism* (New York, 1930).

5. Cf. O. Cox, *Caste, Class and Race* (New York, 1948).

6. Cf. Gunnar Myrdal, *An American Dilemma: The Negro Problem and Modern Democracy*, 20th edition (New York, 1962), pp. 97–112.

7. Cf. W. Graham Sumner, *Folkways: A Study of the Sociological Importance of Usages, Manners, Customs, Mores and Morals* (New York, 1906).

8. Cf. Franklin H. Giddings, *Studies in the Theory of Human Society* (New York, 1922).

9. Cf. *Notes of a Native Son* (Boston, 1957; London, 1964); *Nobody Knows My Name* (New York, 1961; London, 1964); *The Fire Next Time* (New York and London, 1963).

10. Patrick Keatley, "Sex and Settlers," in *The Politics of Partnership* (London, 1963), p. 251 seq.

11. Colin Morris, in his autobiography *The Hour After Midnight*, quoted in Keatley, *op. cit.*, pp. 264–265. The whole question of miscegenation is discussed at length in Chapter IX.

12. Foley, *op. cit.*, p. 626.

13. Cf. R. A. Schermerhorn, *These Our People: Minorities in American Culture* (Boston, 1949).

14. Cf. Robert MacIver, *The More Perfect Union* (New York, 1948).

15. Ashley Montague, *Man in Process* (New York, 1962), p. 102.

16. Cf. L. F. Buckley in *The Catholic Mind* (1962), No. 1163.

17. William J. Kenealy, "Racism: A God-Damned Thing," in *The Catholic Mind*, LXI (1963), No. 1177, 27.

18. A. H. Richmond, *op. cit.*, p. 20.

19. Cf. Margery Perham, *The Colonial Reckoning* (London, 1963), pp. 77–79. A rather full and very interesting account of the English slave trade can be found in *The Observer* (London), magazine section, for Sunday, October 17, 1965, by Hugh Thomas.

20. Cf. Eric Williams, *Capitalism and Slavery* (University of North Carolina, 1944), p. 126.

21. *Op. cit.*, pp. 79–80.

22. Cf. Richmond, *op. cit.*, p. 217.

23. Quoted in Keatley, *op. cit.*, p. 75.

24. Cf. Colin McGlashan, "Integrating Britain's anti-Racialists," in *The Observer*, January 24, 1965. You also have the National Federation of Pakistani Associations, the London West Indian Standing Conference, the Universal Coloured People's Association, and the

Racial Adjustment Action Society. Cf. *The Sunday Times*, 29 October, 1967.

25. Sheila Patterson, *Dark Strangers* (London, 1963).

26. *The Times*, January 27, 1965.

27. Cf. report "Wilson hits out at Colour Bar," in *The Observer*, December 13, 1964.

28. Cf. *The Sunday Times*, December 6, 1964.

29. Cf. Anthony Cronin's article, "MP's unite to amend Race Bill," in *The Sunday Times*, April 11, 1965. Cf. also *The Sunday Times*, 5 November, 1967.

30. Cf. Sir John Fischer Williams, *Some Aspects of the Covenant of the League of Nations* (Oxford, 1934).

31. Cited in *ibid.*, pp. 190–191.

32. Cf. *The Sunday Times*, April 11, 1965.

33. Published in *New Society*, July, 1964.

For Further Reading

E. M. Baker, "Do We teach Racial Intolerance?" in *The Historical Outlook*, XXIV (1933), 86–89.

Michael Banton, *The Coloured Quarter*, London, 1955.

———, *White and Coloured*, London, 1959.

S. Collins, *Coloured Minorities in Britain*, London, 1957.

John Dollard, and others, *Frustration and Aggression*, New Haven, 1939.

Joyce Eggington, *They Seek a Living*, London, 1957.

Ruth Glass, *Newcomers*, London, 1960.

C. S. Hill, *West Indian Migrants and the London Churches*, Oxford, 1963.

Guy Hunter (ed.), *Industrialisation and Race Relations*, London, 1965.

B. Lasker, *Race Attitudes in Children*, New York, 1929.

Colin Legum, "Colour—The Age-old Conflict," in *The Observer*, 10 March, 1968.

Sidney Olivier, "Colour Prejudice," in *The Contemporary Review*, CXXI (1923).

James Pope-Hennessy, *Sins of the Fathers*, London, 1967.

H. Powdermaker, *Probing Our Prejudices*, New York, 1944.

A. Richmond, *Colour Prejudice in Britain*, London, 1954.

Arnold Rose, *The Roots of Prejudice*, Paris, 1951.

S. K. Ruck (ed.), *The West Indian Comes to England*, London, 1960.

James Wickenden, *Colour in Britain*, Oxford, 1958.

CHAPTER V

Racial Discrimination: The U.S.A. and Britain

In contradistinction to race prejudice, racial discrimination is an objective thing. It consists in ["positive acts of deprivation directed towards the members of another ethnic group, individually or collectively."[1] It is a form of non-violent coercion aimed at enforcing certain status relationships by means of social, economic or political distinctions.

Racial discrimination does not necessarily mean the status subordination of minorities to the majority. Undoubtedly it can and sometimes does take this form, but it can also mean the subordination of the majority to a minority. When this happens discrimination tends to be intense and extreme because the situation is likely to be unstable by reason of the minority being unsure of itself. Indeed it can easily lead to open conflict and violent coercion, as is the case today in certain parts of Africa between Europeans and non-Europeans. On the other hand, when the two groups are more or less equal in numbers we find that social separation or segregation is resorted to, rather than racial discrimination as such.

Negroes in the United States

For many years the situation of the Negro in the United States has provided a perfect example of racial discrimination.[2] The entire history of the Negro American is relevant to the question. Today there are over 19,000,000 Negroes in the United States. While the ancestors of some may have come to the country even before Columbus, the vast majority were brought to the States forcibly during the days of the slave traffic. This began shortly after the year 1441, the date of the first Portuguese West African expedition. During the early sixteenth century the king of Portugal carried on a lucrative trade supplying Negro slaves to Europe, while the Spaniards brought them to the West Indies and Central America. About 1535 the Portuguese began sending them to Brazil. During this period also, as we have seen, England began to take part in the business as a profitable commercial transaction. It was shortly after this that North America began to import slaves, through the Spanish and Dutch, an importation that developed to a big volume at the end of the eighteenth century when the use of the cotton gin made it possible to increase cotton production in the South. It continued until after the Civil War when it was abolished.

From this time on, due to various influences, the civic position of Negro Americans generally improved. By 1870 the effects of the previous condition of slavery had been largely done away with and all had the right to vote. Loopholes, however, were availed of, particularly in the South, to nullify this right in practice. Qualifications pertaining to literacy or the possession of property, for example, were effectively used to prevent its exercise by many Negroes.

This was the beginning of a political discrimination against the Negro, many vestiges of which remain even today. Over the years it has taken more subtle and refined forms. Not all forms, however, were subtle and refined. For example, after it had been found that the literacy and property qualifications were succeeding in disenfranchising not only Negroes but some of the poorer and less educated whites, the "Grandfather Clause" was introduced, whereby only persons whose ancestors had the vote before 1867 were entitled to enjoy it now. This was clearly designed to exclude the Negroes.

A historical account of the betterment of the Negroes' position through federal legislation will be summarized in the following chapter. It is a process by which their condition has passed gradually from slavery to full-fledged citizenship. The Civil Rights Act of 1964 represents its culmination. Despite it all, however, discrimination against them can still be found. In the South, especially, the old ideas die hard. By mid-1965 in Alabama only 24 percent of Negroes of voting age had their names on the election registers, as compared with 70 percent of potential white voters. In the "Black Belt"—the southern and central parts of the State, including Montgomery and Selma—full Negro voting registration could almost cause a political revolution. And it is here particularly that registrars have been accustomed to insist on a literacy test designed to disqualify applicants of lower educational levels. In those places where registrars were not required to give reasons why an applicant had failed, the opportunity for discrimination is evident.

It is true that the situation has improved even since 1965, due mainly, perhaps, to the special voting rights bill, signed by President Johnson in August of that year. This bill, by making sure that there will be no effective way of refusing the entitled Negro his voting right, almost immediately added more than a million Negroes to the voting rolls. In fact by mid-1966 there had been an increase of more than 50 percent in the Negro vote in the South, a phenomenon that would have been undreamed of a year or two before. But while this is sufficient in a few areas to give Negroes a voice in local politics, it is far from enabling them to play any significant part in swaying national elections, even a part proportionate to their total numbers in the community.

Of course racial discrimination can take many forms other than political.[3] In the past especially, and again in the South, we find various kinds of educational discrimination. Negroes have been excluded from many public schools and, at the same time, have not been given a fair quota of their own schools. In some States where they constitute 50 percent of the population they have at times received only about 10 percent of the expenditure on education. In the economic field also they have been subjected to many varieties of discrimination. Sometimes Negroes have simply been refused work; sometimes they have been given only work of inferior kinds. Sometimes they have been given lower rates of pay than other workers; sometimes they have been excluded from trade unions. In the matter of housing, Negroes have frequently been restricted as regards choice of residence, sometimes by law, sometimes by opposition from white property holders. In the field of recreation, discrimination has been particularly severe, many recreational centers—some even publicly owned—being barred to Negroes. There has also been discrimination in other public places, inferior accommodation being accorded to them in restaurants, trains, buses, hospitals and even churches. Frequently they are charged the same prices as the whites pay for the better accommodation accorded to them. Such forms of discrimination can still be found in places in spite of all efforts to date to eradicate them.

Ethical Principles Governing Discrimination

From the ethical point of view, one guiding principle concerning racial discrimination was enunciated by Monsignor John Ireland, archbishop of St. Paul, in 1891, on the anniversary of the abolition of slavery. He asserted that while unfair discrimination is always unlawful, not all discrimination is necessarily unjust. A British authority on the color problem, Anthony Richmond, has said similarly, "it should be noted that there is a subtle but important distinction between differentiation or discrimination *between* and discrimination *against*."[4]

What we have here referred to as "unfair discrimination" is not that which distinguishes between one group in the community and another, but rather that which enhances the power and privileges of a "superordinate" (Richmond) status group at the expense of the subordinate. This is the type of discrimination which is usually meant when people speak simply of "racial discrimination." And in this sense it cannot be defended as moral. Nevertheless, from the point of view of academic ethical theory, there can be a form of discrimination—in the sense of differentiation between rather than discrimination against—which is not necessarily immoral and which can be of relevance, even in matters affecting race relations.

But the majority of discriminatory practices mentioned in connection with the Negro American do seem to be open to the charge of injustice. Those in the educational field seem to be not only inequitable here and now, but also to serve to perpetuate the inability of the Negro to assume full participation in society. Those in the economic field seem more often than not to be based on insufficient grounds. The fact is that whites are not always superior workers; surveys have shown that Negroes are better or as good as whites in efficiency and regularity of attendance. Nor is the existence of anti-Negro prejudice on the part of white workers an adequate reason for the exclusion of Negroes by employers or unions. A combination of the closed shop and closed union could, theoretically at least, mean a denial of the human right to work. For it is obvious that if a particular work place is closed to all except members of one particular union, and if, at the same time, that union is closed to all but white workers, the Negro is deprived of the possibility of finding work there.

Discrimination in the housing field has also frequently been unjust, again largely because it is founded on inadequate reasons which cause particular individuals to suffer because of objections bearing on the group. Fear of depreciation following Negro occupancy is the most common reason for discrimination in the matter of housing. In the recreational sector, forms of discrimination such as those mentioned above are very unfair to children, leading frequently to stunted development and a penchant for crime.

But discrimination in the field of work is probably the most harmful kind. Contrary to the popular impression, the Negro's economic position relative to that of the white man has actually deteriorated over the last ten years. Recent studies have shown that the unemployment level of Negroes has always been above the white level. It was 64 percent higher in 1947, 92 percent higher in 1952, 124 percent higher in 1962, and again 124 percent higher in 1964.[5] Figures for 1966 reveal that the general Negro unemployment rate is twice that of whites, and the average pay less than half. Half of America's unemployed teenagers are Negro, although they represent only 15 percent of the population in this age group.[6]

To a certain extent Negroes are managing to ascend the social ladder. Between 1955 and 1962 they registered substantial gains in the professional and educational services. Still in 1962 only 17 percent of all employed non-whites were in white collar occupations as compared to 47 percent of white employees. Only 4 percent were in the professions as against 11 percent of whites, and only 2.7 percent were proprietors as against 14.6 percent. Differences in earnings, too, are quite appreciable. Thus in 1962 the median annual wage of a white male worker was $4,569, as against $2,652 in the case of a Negro; that of a white woman worker was $2,364 as against $1,055 in the case of her colored counterpart.[7]

Further surveys have sketched the pattern for the immediate future. They show that Negroes can expect some advances in certain sectors. For example during the period to 1970 there should be a 27 percent rate of growth in their participation in white collar jobs. But this represents their biggest potential advance. The general picture continues to be one of discrimination. To quote from one of the surveys utilized here: "It appears, . . . that the restrictions and competition for admission to apprenticeship programs, especially in the building trades, may continue to affect adversely the Negro's opportunities for major gains in these areas. This is a serious situation, as it denies Negroes the opportunity to enter the most rapidly expanding industry."[8]

The general upshot of these developments is a growing consciousness of the fact that civil rights advances in the recent present and near future have benefited, and are likely to benefit, the minority more than the masses. While Negroes have for the first time come to secure appointments to the president's cabinet and a leading national bank, and to take part in activities long barred to members of their race, the situation of the poorer Negroes continues to grow worse. Some 44 percent of them are crowded into slums, as against 13 percent in the case of whites. It is the emerging Negro middle class that has benefited to date by the "Negro revolution," not the Negro masses. And the question is: How long will the Negro masses be content with this situation?

The Negro masses in question are by no means confined to the South. The contrary in fact is the case. While the civil rights legislation passed under President Johnson has somewhat eased the tensions in the South, it has scarcely affected the situation of Negroes in the North. It matters little to the dwellers in the crowded ghettoes of Harlem that they are legally entitled to equal education with whites, equal job opportunities, freedom to live where they like, and so on. The fact is that they are, and continue to remain, slum dwellers, with children in inferior schools, and severely handicapped in the struggle of life. They are dogged both by the inertia which impedes the progress of all deprived groups, and by an ever-ready and sometimes violent white reaction to their betterment. The reaction of sections of whites in Philadelphia and Brooklyn during the Summer of 1966 is typical of what the Negro faces in the North. It took the rather ironical form of creating an organization called SPONGE—the "Society for the Prevention of Negroes Getting Everything."

The Race Policies of American and British Trade Unions

Discrimination against the Negro by trade unions has been a feature of the American scene since the period beginning around 1885. It was this period which saw the appearance of a trend towards the exclusion of colored workers from the skilled trades. But the tendency spread quickly to more general unions, and the American Federation of Labor, which had its origin about this time, has been affected by it since. Thus H. R. Northrup, in a study of the relations between organized labor and the Negroes, writes: "The trend became institutionalized in the new unions of the period. Clauses excluding all but 'Caucasian' workers were inserted in the constitutions of a great majority of the AFL unions. Preemption of the skilled trades by the unionists assigned the Negroes to the unskilled 'helper' work in vast areas of the construction industry and the services and trades. Some railroad unions resorted to violence to exclude Negroes from what were formerly 'Negro jobs' during the depression."[9] We read that over twenty Negro engine firemen were shot on Southern railroads between the years 1931 and 1934.

In more recent years the rise of the Conference of Industrial Organization has actively encouraged the integration of Negroes into union ranks and industries, even calling on management to modify its hiring policies in some instances. By contrast, some AFL unions still seek to maintain their old policy, but are finding it more and more difficult to do so.[10] In fact, due to pressure from the CIO, one of the largest AFL unions—the International Association of Machinists, with a membership of over half a million—has had to change its policy towards Negroes. Indeed by 1949 only one union was left which excluded Negroes by its constitutional provisions, while one other provided separate local unions for colored workers.

But in actual practice the provision of separate and segregated local unions for Negro workers still endures in many AFL branches. One American moralist has castigated this practice as involving "more than a merely technical division of the union into two locals; it also implies a whole program of discrimination with regard to jobs in which the Negro locals are given the leavings after the white locals have had their pick of job opportunities. Work permits issued by the unions are carefully restricted and controlled."[11]

In Britain for quite a number of years the question of the employment of foreign workers in general has been a live issue in agriculture and coal mining. Although the agriculture unions have been the most bitterly opposed to the employment of foreign workers, due to a shortage of labor many of them have in fact been placed in agricultural occupations. For the same reason the National Union of Mineworkers has come to accept foreign workers, albeit with reluctance. But because many British miners refuse to work with them, recruitment has had to be abandoned.

Few British unions have any formal policy on the question of the employment of colored workers. However, in 1955 the Transport and General Workers Union called upon the government to work out a policy based on a control of immigration and the provision of increased capital investment in the colonies, particularly the West Indies, so as to provide work and decent living conditions for the people there, thus eliminating the need to emigrate.

In Britain the major union problem is to be found in the craft unions, which sometimes do not accept the qualifications of immigrant workers. The problem arises from the fact that if a union card cannot be produced, work cannot normally be secured. For on their part, employers frequently make union membership a condition of employment, while "redundancy clauses" stipulate that in the case of unemployment foreign workers should be the first to be dismissed. Admittedly these clauses have not been rigidly followed in practice, British and foreign workers being laid off in proportionate numbers wherever necessary. Nevertheless, it is fair to say that the fear of problems arising from unemployment constitutes the major problem in the way of the employment of colored workers in Britain.[12]

Discrimination—Hen or Egg?

Both in Britain and the United States—and particularly in the latter country—the chief reason given in defense of discrimination against colored people in every field is their allegedly high degree of unsocial and anti-social behavior. In their defense it has been argued in turn that, in so far as they are in fact characterized by such behavior, it is due to white discrimination against them in the past which has given them no chance to enjoy a normal social development. In this vein it is argued that the high Negro crime rate in America is primarily a result of prejudice and poverty.

However, while there are many who defend this position strongly, arguing that if discrimination ceased their behavior would improve, quite a number of others see the reason for the unsocial behavior of Negro Americans as stemming from the high degree of their social disorganization. Three instances of this have been underlined. Firstly, the Negro American lacks the social support of strong traditional family loyalties such as were possessed by European peasant immigrants to the United States. Secondly, the American Negro community does not have as strong institutions of social organization (e.g., recreational groups, etc.) as the Europeans had to help them in the acculturation process. Thirdly, until the recent emergence of people like Martin Luther King, there has been a greater social distance between Negro leadership—predominantly middle class—and the Negro masses than there ever was among European immigrants to America. Due to the existence of these factors, it has been argued that apart altogether from the existence of discrimination, the Negro community has been incapable of developing a high degree of social performance.

However, the debate continues. In 1965, Charles E. Silberman published an important contribution to it, entitled significantly *Crisis in Black and White.* In contrast with Gunnar Myrdal's study in the 1940's, *An American Dilemma,* which made it the orthodox thing to do to assume that the problem of the Negro American is at heart a white problem (an assumption, as we have seen, that is also made by James Baldwin), Silberman emphasizes the sickness of the Negro community itself. The situation is not such that everything will be all right if only the white man would undergo a change of heart. Only the Negro himself can make himself equal, and here he is up against a problem. For, as Silberman puts it, "part of the price of being a Negro in America is a degree of paranoia."

If Negroes are to be helped by white men, it must be by way of being helped to help themselves. But this again requires that they be supplied with ordinary amenities. One American Jesuit concludes his examination of the matter as follows:

> It is obvious from our analysis that action is necessary to better prepare the Negro to take advantage of expanding economic opportunities. Students of the problem seem to agree that the basic reasons for the inability of the Negro to qualify for more skilled and higher-level jobs, even if he had complete equality of opportunity, are related to low incomes, lack of family interest in advanced education, inadequate housing, low quality and segregated schooling, and inadequate vocational guidance.[13]

Whatever the outcome of this debate, one thing is certainly clear: racial discrimination, while it may be morally permissible if it is simply discrimination between and not at all discrimination against, is something which almost always tends to be unjust. One has always to balance the reasonable motives of the discriminating group with its potentially unfair consequences for any of the groups being discriminated between. Such balancing of interests is never an easy task. For if it is true to say that discrimination almost always becomes unfair, it is also true that there could exist circumstances in which failure to discriminate would be equally unfair to the community in general. What must be avoided are not only harsh and unethical attitudes in favor of discrimination, but also the correspondingly unethical and un-realistic attitude of extreme liberalism. One matter of principle alone is clear: in so far as racial discrimination is ever unjust, that is, discrimination against any racial group, it ought to have no place in a Christian community.

Notes

1. A. H. Richmond, *The Colour Problem* (London, 1955), p. 21.

2. Cf. E. J. Ross, *A Survey of Sociology* (Milwaukee, 1932), pp. 470–474.

3. Cf. Ross, *op. cit.*, pp. 476–483.

4. *Op. cit.*, p. 353.

5. Cf. Louis F. Buckley, "Jobs and the Negro," in *The Catholic Mind*, LXII (1964), No. 1180.

6. Cf. Joyce Egginton, "Ghettoes on the Brink," in *The Observer* (London), August 28, 1966.

7. Cf. *ibid.*, "Discriminatory Practices in the Labor Market," in *The Catholic Mind* (1962), No. 1163.

8. *Ibid.*

9. *Organized Labor and the Negro* (New York, 1944).

10. A. Foley, "Minorities in American Society," in *Social Orienta-tions* (St. Louis, 1956), p. 614.

11. Foley, *op. cit.*, p. 615.

12. Cf. R. P. Walsh, "The British Story of Immigrants," in *Migra-tion News* (1962), No. 2.

13. L. F. Buckley, in *The Catholic Mind* (1962), No. 1163.

For Further Reading

R. S. Baker, *Following the Color Line: American Negro Citizenship in the Progressive Era*, New York, 1964.

Nicholas Deakin (ed.), *Colour and the British Electorate*, London, 1965.

John Dollard, *Caste and Class in a Southern Town*, New Haven, 1937.

Mary Gardner, *Deep South: A Social Anthropological Study of Caste and Class*, Chicago, 1941.

J. F. Gilligan, *The Morality of the Color Line*, Washington, 1928.

E. Ginzberg, *The Troublesome Presence: American Democracy and the Negro*, New York, 1964.

R. Hooper, ed., *Colour in Britain*, London, no date.

H. R. Isaacs, *The New World of American Negroes*, Massachusetts, 1964.

Kenneth Little, *Negroes in Britain*, London, 1947.

Charles F. Mardin, *Minorities in American Society*, New York, 1952.

T. F. Pettigrew, *A Profile of the American Negro*, Princeton, 1964.

Janet Reid, "Employment of Negroes in Manchester," in *Sociological Review*, IV (1956), No. 5.

J. Red and R. Moore, *Race, Community and Conflict*, Oxford, 1967.

A. Richmond, "Recent Research on Race Relations in Britain," in *International Social Science Bulletin*, X (1958), No. 3.

Henri Tajfil and John L. Dawson, *Disappointed Guests*, London, 1965.

L. J. Twomey, S.J., *How to think about Race*, St. Louis, 1951.

D. Wilner, and others, *The Housing Environment and Family Life*, Baltimore, 1962.

J. Milton Yinger, *Racial and Cultural Minorities*, New York, 1953.

CHAPTER VI

Racial Segregation: The U.S.A. and South Africa

The theoretical aim behind racial segregation or separation—or *apartheid* as it is called in South Africa—is the avoidance of conflict between two or more racial groups by ensuring that each maintains its own cultural autonomy. Racial segregation may be partial or complete, and may affect many of the matters mentioned in connection with discrimination. Thus segregation can exist in the matter of housing, the use of certain amenities, participation in certain kinds of work, and even representation in government and the civil service.

Although it might be argued in theory that, as such, segregation along racial lines does not necessarily imply discrimination against any racial group, in practice, the one almost always involves the other. It is theoretically possible that all the groups concerned might be in favor of segregation one from the other and might, in fact, resist the breaking down of barriers between them. In such circumstances the maintenance of segregation can be a just and wise policy, and it is in this perspective that it has been defended in the past as necessary in parts of the United States. Thus in 1932 the sociologist Eva Ross wrote: "In the South . . . continued separation seems advisable for the continuance of peace and well-being." She added immediately: "Separation, however, does not mean discrimination. To maintain the public peace, the state has a right to impose restrictions on its citizens, but all the citizens must be affected equally. The restrictions must not be to the detriment of one particular group alone."[1]

Segregation in the United States

The evolution of the Negro's position in the United States may be said to have begun with the issuing on January 1, 1863, of President Lincoln's Emancipation Proclamation. This, together with the fourteenth amendment to the Constitution, approved on December 18, 1865, provided the corner-stone of later Negro legal rights. The fourteenth amendment, with its clause concerning "the equal protection of the laws," affirmed the principle of the universal equality of all citizens of the United States.

The assumption that Negroes enjoyed such equality was confirmed in 1898 by the famous Plessy vs. Ferguson decision. This arose out of a challenge in the courts to a Louisiana statute which required railroads to provide "equal but separate" accommodation for white and colored people. The decision upheld the statute as legal, and in doing so formulated what came to be called the doctrine of "separate but equal" treatment. This implied that the mere fact of segregation in itself did not necessarily involve any inequality or discrimination.

In 1954, however, the Supreme Court, dealing with the question of school segregation, reversed the Plessy vs. Ferguson judgment. Declaring that experience of school segregation had showed that it necessarily involved inequality and therefore some discrimination, the 1954 decision thereby repudiated constitutional justification for segregation of any kind whatsoever. Thus the idea of "separate but equal" was declared a practical impossibility.

But the decision was far from being widely implemented. In certain parts of the country, notably the South, things were pretty much the same even ten years later. Hence the trouble in 1963 and 1964. "At the beginning of 1963," writes Martin Luther King, "nine years after this historic decision, approximately nine percent of Southern Negro students were attending integrated schools. If this pace were maintained, it would be the year 2054 before integration in Southern schools would be a reality."[2]

The schools issue, coupled with that of voting registration, provided the proximate stimuli for President Kennedy's civil rights bill. This represented a federal effort to eliminate segregation in the individual States, which to date managed to maintain it by way of a variety of stratagems. Thus school segregation in the South continued to be practiced, not in virtue of a formal system of racially segregated education, but in virtue of a public placement law, which was designed to arrange the assignment of pupils to schools in accordance with what was deemed to be the best interests of the community. The civil rights bill was also intended to combat neglect of the common law by privately owned units of public accommodation, educational and otherwise, which were wont to refuse entry or service to colored people. In underlining the force of the common law in this respect, the new bill did not confer a federal right to enter such places, but made it a federal offense to refuse to serve anyone in them by reason simply of the color of his skin.

The federal government passed the Civil Rights Act in July, 1964. In many places it has already contributed substantially towards the emergence of a new pattern of race relations. In some areas, this had already begun. A good example is that of Memphis, Tennessee, the cotton capital of the old Confederate South. In Memphis racial integration has gone ahead in an orderly fashion since 1961, when the city was the scene of lawsuits, sit-ins, picketing and other demonstrations. Owing particularly to the Memphis Committee on Community Relations, integration there has gone well beyond the token stage and deep-seated social patterns are being altered. It is reported that Negroes are being appointed to official positions; higher level jobs are opening up for them, and the city and county schools are being desegregated. Negroes and whites serve side by side in the city police force; they attend the same movie theaters and eat at the same restaurants. Similar progress is recorded in the field of public transport and accommodation.[3]

The same things cannot be said of all areas, as the troubles following on the passing of the Civil Rights Act attest. Some of these difficulties have been created by Negroes themselves as, for example, in a number of Eastern cities and in Chicago during the Summer of 1964, and again in the Summer of 1965 in Los Angeles. On the other hand, examples of white violence occurred during the Summer of 1966 in places like Philadelphia, Chicago and Cicero, Illinois.

In December, 1964, a Mississippi court gave proof of a flagrant travesty of justice in failing to react adequately to the death during the previous June of three civil rights workers at the hands of an anti-Negro faction. It was after this, in January, 1965, that Dr. Martin Luther King began his now famous civil rights drive. The launching took place in Selma, Alabama. Selma was a place that had been intransigent on the issue of desegregation since the 1954 Supreme Court decision on the matter. It had resisted integration in every domain. Hence Dr. King's effort at organized registration of Negroes on hotel registers and voting lists in Selma. Hence, too, his arrangement of the much publicized Negro march from Selma to Montgomery, the county capital.

For all this, not one single extra Negro voter was registered. But in the long run the campaign may have been efficacious, particularly by way of stirring the conscience of the nation. It may well be that it had some influence on the putting through of the special voting rights bill by President Johnson in 1965. But even these gains suffered in 1966 when a resurgence of "white backlash" together with the threat of "black power" led to the defeat of a further civil rights bill which had a controversial "open housing" section.

Apartheid in South Africa

The same process is occurring in South Africa over *apartheid*, the full enormity of which is only slowly coming to be realized. Separate development was the brain-child of the late Dr. Verwoerd who, realizing that full political partition might easily be suicidal, conceived the idea of having the Africans live in semi-independent territories (termed Bantustans), eight of which were to be developed. Towards this end, a number of native reserves were set aside which the Africans might leave for daily work, but which they were not to leave without a pass. Although to date only one Bantustan—the Transkei experiment—has been created, the whole system of reserves has fallen into disrepute.

In this matter concrete instances speak volumes. Leslie Rubin has provided forty examples of what the South African set-up can do to human beings.[4] It must suffice to produce but one of these here. It is that no African, lawfully residing in a town by virtue of a permit issued to him, is entitled, as of right, to have his wife and children residing with him. The whole business of work permits is insufferable. Every year more than 40,000 non-white South Africans fall within the category of pass-law offenders by reason of entering white territory for purposes of work without a permit. The proof and the offense are identical, in that if one is an African and has left one's papers at home, then one has *ipso facto* committed a crime. Then there are the Immorality Amendment Act of 1950 and the Mixed Marriages Act of 1959, in virtue of which not only marriage but extra-marital sex relations are prohibited between Europeans and non-Europeans.[5]

Apartheid extends even to the sphere of the theater, the South African government having passed a law forbidding Europeans to play to mixed audiences.[6] In fact the Publications and Entertainments Act, which set up a Publications Control Board, has led to considerable literary censorship in the name of *apartheid*.

For example, during the Summer of 1966, a novel by the South African novelist Nadine Gordimer, *The Late Bourgeois World*, was banned by reason, it is understood, of the objection of the censors to scenes of social mixing of the races portrayed in it. There seem to be very few sectors of life which are not affected by the implications of *apartheid*.

Objections to the System of Apartheid

Apart altogether from the question of ethics, the system of *apartheid* in South Africa is confronted with many practical difficulties. For one thing, it is quite unrealistic to seek to effect a simple twofold division of South Africans into Bantus and people of white racial stock. In so far as race has meaning at all, there are many races among the black Africans themselves. From the biometric point of view, there are three main racial groups—the Bushman, the Negro and the Hamite—while further divisions stem from differing cultural traits, especially language.

In addition, there is the difficulty that the population includes at least 1,700,000 "coloreds," that is, people of mixed racial descent. In 1965 a new political party claiming the Western Cape Province and Namaqualand as the exclusive national home of this colored element was launched in Cape Town. This idea of a "Coloredstan" corresponds to the government's policy of Bantustans for the Africans proper, except that the new party is to insist on real sovereignty in the Coloredstan. In fact it aims at total geographic, political, economic, constitutional, cultural and social independence in its true sense, with no leaning on white South Africa—except in reciprocal agreements between the Republic and other countries, especially in the matter of external defense.

One wonders what process may be selected for testing applications for "citizenship" of this Coloredstan. Even in the present state of things such criteria are sadly lacking when it comes to a matter of deciding whether a man is black or white. Enlistment in the army of Rhodesia and Nyasaland, for example, has been confined to applicants who are "physically fit in all respects and British subjects of pure European descent." "One wonders," says a commentator on this, "what scientific processes are invoked as the potential recruits line up for their ethnic test. British subject, born in Soho of Italian parentage... suspiciously dark skin. Hmm. Application claiming Welsh parentage. Crinkly hair. Fingernails not quite right. Birthplace given as Cardiff. Tiger Bay? British subject, born Kuala Lumpur, claims father was an engineer in the colonial service. Eyelids funny, suggest recheck..."[7]

This is the sort of thing that leads inevitably to population registers, race classification boards and the like. But *apartheid* is impracticable in quite a number of other respects due to the vital part played by Africans in business and commerce. In 1946, for example, they represented 29 percent of those employed in commerce, 33 percent of those employed in transport and communications, 47 percent of those employed in the manufacturing industries and 89 percent of those employed in mining and quarrying. For the same reason *apartheid* is clearly impractical in the domains of housing, education and politics.

Of course, if a man wants to escape from this world of work and business, he can always go into one of the native reserves—areas of land set aside for the Bantus as a step forward furthering eventual geographical *apartheid*. In these reserves farming is virtually the only industry, and since the Union of South Africa lives off the gold industry rather than off agriculture, putting the Africans into such reserves tends to decrease their economic importance and power. But it is also undesirable from the point of view of the economy as a whole. Most areas of the Union are interdependent. Indeed it was originally founded chiefly in the interest of fostering an economic co-operation that was understood to be necessary. With geographic *apartheid*, trade famines could develop, commerce be cramped and defense made considerably more difficult.[8]

And yet, despite all this, white South Africans as a whole cling tenaciously to a policy of at least some form of *apartheid*. They are not the only people who have thought of *apartheid* in connection with Africa. It was in the context of Africa that Hitler said in 1936: "The white race is destined to rule."[9] In the event of German victory a policy of *apartheid* would have been imposed on the Africans, at least in the recovered former German African territories.[10] But the white South Africans have worked out their own ethos of *apartheid*, articulated, internally logical, cogent up to a point, worthy of study and of at least some appreciation.

An understanding of the broad lines of this ethos is necessary to an understanding of South Africa. The Afrikaners are convinced that they are confronted with a serious problem. The fact is that their civilization is profoundly different from that of the Bantu and also, incidentally, that of the modern "Coca-Cola society." "Their roots go back to the Bible and the Calvinism of the seventeenth century; they think of the farm and the ox-wagon and the open veld, the old self-sufficient patriarchal existence. There are still many women in Johannesburg who dare not appear at home on the farm wearing trousers or lipstick; there are still families where hardly any book is seen but the Bible; the predikant is still a man of great influence."[11]

A Theological Defense of Racial Segregation

The Dutch Reformed Church has worked out an entire theological position that is not only consistent with, but demands the system of *apartheid*.[12] In 1950 a meeting of the Dutch Reformed Churches held in Bloemfontein approved of complete separation as an ideal. Its conclusions were that a policy of "eventual intermingling" (i.e. desegregation) "is rejected because it will lead to unnecessary clashes between the two races, will dig the grave for the future of the white race, and will therefore be a great disadvantage for Christian culture in Africa." In place of it the meeting defended an *apartheid* policy of complete segregation as something which should be worked towards in the future.[13]

The interesting thing is that the government did not adopt this policy, for it called for far too many white sacrifices. In particular, the whites would be required to do much of the manual labor that at present is being furnished by the blacks. Hence, when the Churches met again, an alternative policy was put forward. This involved a modified form of segregation, the blacks coming to work in Union territory in a migratory or commuting fashion, and without being provided with facilities for development within their own reserves. Although stoutly resisted by a minority as being incompatible with the Christian ethic, this policy was adopted and is still in force.

However, there is indeed a minority view of the matter in the Dutch Reformed Church. Thus, speaking at Pretoria in 1953, Professor B. B. Keet of the Stellenbosch Theological College protested: "There is only one *apartheid* known to Scripture and that is separation from sin."[14] The dominating idea of the Reformed Church is very different. It is supremely conscious of the importance of distinctiveness and hence of separate groups, because of the fact that, as it sees things, in both the Old and the New Testaments the Holy Spirit reveals himself by working outwards in concentric rings from a small center. He always uses secure bases of righteousness for the purpose of communicating the Christian life to the infidel. They invoke St. Paul, 2 Corinthians 6:14–17: "Be ye not yoked together with unbelievers: for what fellowship hath righteousness with unrighteousness . . . Wherefore come out from among them, and be ye separate, saith the Lord."

In other words, in order to be useful to the unconverted, the Afrikan must retain his own separate identity. Speaking at Pretoria, the Reverend C. B. Brink, moderator of a Reformed

Church of the Transvaal and chairman of the Federation of Dutch Reformed Churches of South Africa, said: "To create a cosmos, God separated things: light from darkness, waters above the firmament from waters under the firmament, dry land from sea. All living creatures too . . . No uniformity without differences, therefore, but a multiplicity containing rich diversity, such is the way of creation. To ignore difference is to build another Tower of Babel."[15]

In particular, one must not understand the unity of Christians in the mystical body of Christ as being of such a kind as to destroy all other differences. As Dr. J. C. Kotze put it, speaking at Johannesburg: "Making them one in a Christian sense does not destroy their identity as peoples. That they remain Jews, Greeks, Romans and so on, makes no difference to this unity." Which reminds one of Luther's dictum, in a pamphlet against the Peasants' Revolt, to the effect that "the unity and equality of the blood of Christ is spiritual and not social." Allied to this is the idea that the Christian religion is not a religion of social reform. This has been expressed as follows by Dr. Jansen, the governor general of the Union of South Africa: "I think I am right in saying that neither Christ nor the Apostles ever went beyond the preaching of the gospel of salvation and warning against wrong attitudes of mind. I do not think that they ever concerned themselves with the politics of the day."[16]

Let us conclude this section with one final quotation, an official pronouncement of the Dutch Reformed Church:

> Every nation and race will be able to perform the greatest service to God and the world if it keeps its own national attributes, received from God's own hand, pure with honor and gratitude . . . God divides humanity into races, languages and nations. Differences are not only willed by God but are perpetuated by him. Equality between natives, coloreds and Europeans includes a misappreciation of the fact that God in his providence made people into different races and nations . . . Far from the word of God encouraging equality, it is an established scriptural principle that

in every community ordination there is a fixed relationship
between authorities . . . Those who are culturally and spiritu-
ally advanced have a mission of leadership and protection of the
less advanced . . . The natives must be led and formed towards
independence so that eventually they will be equal to the Europeans, but each on their own territory and each serving God and
their fatherland.[17]

Allowing for some criticism of these sentiments which has
been made by several Dutch Reformed predikants, by and large
they represent the theological view that is accepted by a very
large number of people within that church. Indeed Father Trevor
Huddleston has summed up the situation when he says that the
theology of the Dutch Reformed Church, with its great insistence
on "election," is "the ideally suitable religious doctrine for
white South Africa. It provides at the same moment a moral
justification for white supremacy and an actual, day to day reason
for asserting it."[18]

It is this theology which explains why, in 1954, at the World
Council of Churches, the South African representatives of the
Dutch Reformed Church were able to refuse to give assent to
a declaration which affirmed that any form of social discrimination is contrary to the will of God. In so far as they envisage the
ending of *apartheid* at all, it is in an eschatological context that
is understood as not of our time.

"For God's Sake Wake Up"

In allowing such developments to take place, Father Huddleston
has charged the church with being guilty of a serious apathy.
"The church," he writes, "sleeps on. White Christianity is more
concerned to retain its character of a law-abiding force than to
express its abhorrence of such attacks on personal liberties."[19]
Nor will official pronouncements alone meet the challenge. It is
now much too late for these alone. Huddleston draws an analogy
between this situation and the early years of the Hitler persecution
of the Jews when the official voice of the church was silent: "The

Niemollers and the Faulhabers called too late upon the Christian world."

However, Father Huddleston is optimistic that the church, not simply in the sense of "the hierarchy" but "in its Pauline sense as that living organism which has 'many members,'"-is capable of taking a "prophetic initiative" against the evil that is *apartheid* in South Africa. It is but seldom in history, he avers, that the hierarchy gives evidence of such initiative. A Thomas à Becket or a Faulhaber are conspicuous by reason of their rarity. It is the Christian conscience as such that must awaken. This can happen, but it has not as yet happened in South Africa.[20]

Somewhat the same charges are made in the United States against the Christian churches for holding back from a proper denunciation of the injustice of racial segregation. In May, 1965, in an article in *Look*, Robert W. Spike, director of the National Council of Churches Commission on Religion and Race, soundly castigated the church in general for having "aided and abetted the Anglo-Saxon white conspiracy."[21] It has done this, he maintained, by not having influenced its adherents sufficiently to practice racial justice in such matters as housing, by having practiced discrimination—at least of a limited kind—in its own internal life, and by ignoring in practice its own preaching concerning human equality by being satisfied to work towards racial equality in a merely gradualist fashion.

In Spike's eyes the most damning evidence of this failure of the Christian church in America is the widespread existence of separate Negro denominations. For these have been made necessary by the depth of the rejection with which Negro Christians have had to contend. Similar considerations might be adduced in connection with the growth of West Indian churches in present-day England.[22]

In America one support of segregation has been the biblical literalism of some of the white Christian churches. By way of such literalism, involving ideas such as that the parables of

Scripture are presentations of scientific truth, the curse of Ham is extended (though by what authority no one seems to know) to cover all people of dark skin, while the statement that God has "set the bounds of the habitation of men" is made to serve as a scriptural defense of segregation.

To the extent that any or all of the foregoing may be true, the American Christian churches have something to account for. And it will take more to right the wrong than that clerics wearing black armbands should march in Selma in mourning for the slain civil rights workers.[23] Indeed to the extent that Robert Spike's charge is true, the Christian churches of America must be up and doing if they are to save the allegiance of the Negro. No doubt similar considerations were in the mind of Father Huddleston when, as long ago as August, 1953, he penned his famous letter to a London newspaper with the unusual heading "For God's Sake Wake Up."[24]

Notes

1. *A Survey of Sociology* (Milwaukee, 1932), p. 476.
2. *Why We Can't Wait* (New York, 1963), p. 18.
3. Cf. T. Dalton, "Racial Prejudice is diminishing in the not-so-deep South," in *The Irish Independent*, February 26, 1965.
4. *This is Apartheid* (London, 1960), *passim.*
5. Cf. Trevor Huddleston, *Naught for your Comfort* (London, 1956), pp. 27–28.
6. Cf. "Apartheid Theatres," in *The Sunday Times* (London), April 11, 1965. It was due to difficulties on this score that Peter Shaffer refused permission to allow his play *The Royal Hunt of the Sun* to be produced in South Africa. When the producer, Hymie Udwin, managing director of South Africa's Theatre International, agreed to put the play on before segregated audiences provided the Spaniards were played by whites and the Incas by coloreds, the government introduced new legislation whereby coloreds and whites

were not allowed on the same stage. In addition, in anticipation of trouble from authors, the South African minister for economics announced that he intended to introduce an amendment to the Copyright Act, which would prevent writers from refusing performance of their works on ideological or unreasonable grounds.

7. Patrick Keatley, *The Politics of Partnership* (London, 1963), pp. 252–253.

8. Cf. Roger M. Ricklefs, "Racial Tension in South Africa," in *America*, November 29, 1958.

9. As reported in *The Times*, January 27, 1936.

10. Cf. *Volkischer Beobachter*, January 24, 1939.

11. Philip Mason, *Christianity and Race* (London, 1956), pp. 49–50.

12. Cf. *ibid.*, Part I, Ch. 2, "The Views of the Dutch Reformed Churches."

13. Cf. *ibid.*, p. 52.

14. Cited in *ibid.*, p. 60.

15. Cited in *ibid.*, p. 56.

16. Cited in *ibid.*, p. 57.

17. In Huddleston, *op. cit.*, p. 49.

18. Cf. *ibid.*, p. 51.

19. *Ibid.*, p. 108.

20. *Ibid.*, p. 117.

21. "Our Churches Sin Against the Negro," in *Look*, May 18, 1965.

22. Cf. Malcolm Colley's article in *New Society*, August, 1964.

23. Cf. report "Nuns and Priests on the March," in *The Advocate* of Melbourne, March 18, 1965.

24. Cf. *The Observer*, August 30, 1953.

For Further Reading

Civil Rights U.S.A.: Public Schools North and West, Washington, 1962.

Civil Rights U.S.A.: Public Schools Southern States, Washington, 1962.

Equal Protection of the Laws in North Carolina, Washington, 1959–62.

South Africa and the Rule of Law, Report of the International Commission of Jurists, Geneva, 1960.

The United States Commission on Civil Rights, Washington, 1961.

Robert Birley, "What's Changing in South Africa," in *The Observer*, 23 April, 1967.

R. E. Cushman, *Civil Liberties in the United States*, New York, 1956.

G. Gardiner, "The Treason Trial in South Africa," in *Journal of the International Commission of Jurists*, I (1957), No. 1.

R. W. Gleason, S.J., "Immorality of Segregation," in *The Interracial Review*, XXXIV (1961), 26–35.

Muriel Howell, *A Survey of Race Relations in South Africa, 1957–58*, South African Institute of Race Relations, 1958.

F. P. Spooner, *South African Predicament: The Economics of Apartheid*, New York, 1961.

CHAPTER VII

Race and Immigration: Britain and the U.S.A.

During the course of history there have been many mass movements of population from one part of the globe to another. The nineteenth century, in particular, saw a considerable exodus from Europe to the New World of America. Yet in this matter, as in so many others, the present century has far outstripped its predecessors.

Political and Economic Migration

The figures which describe the refugee movement in post-war Western Europe are quite staggering when their total is computed. West Germany alone has received nearly 10 million refugees, from East Germany and the Soviet Satellites. Austria and France have each absorbed about a quarter of a million, Finland about half a million, East Germany nearly four million and Britain about 300 thousand. The total for other European countries reaches over 200 thousand.[1]

The rest of the world has also received its quota. According to the United Nations high commissioner for refugees, reporting in 1954, there were about 17 million refugees in India and Pakistan, five million in Korea, six and a half million in Japan, one million in Palestine and 750 thousand in Burma. Altogether there are some 40 million people in the world who have been driven from their homes and forced to emigrate. Some of these have settled down in the countries to which they fled; others merely await the opportunity to travel further. They constitute a real problem for certain countries.

The causes of this *political* migration are varied.[2] In the case
of Finland, for example, after the end of the Finnish-Soviet War
in 1944 and the ceding of Karelia and Salla to the U.S.S.R., the
armistice provided for the evacuation of the entire Finnish
population from these territories. In 1950 the last remnants of
the Turkish minority in Bulgaria—some 250 thousand people—
were given three months to leave that country. Following the
Jewish-Arab War and the partition of Palestine, when the Jews
took over an area inhabited by some 350 thousand Arabs, these
latter decided to seek refuge in neighboring countries. Similarly,
following the partition of India and Pakistan, there was a huge
two-way exodus of minority groups seeking to join their co-
religionists on the other side of the frontier. Then, of course,
there is the case of the Japanese, about six million of whom found
it necessary to return to their homeland from all over the Far
East on the termination of the Second World War.

In addition to political migration there is migration that is due
to *economic* causes.[3] It is both intra- and inter-continental in
scope. Within Europe such migration, though large, is mainly
regional and is often of short-term duration. The greater amount
of economic migration is inter-continental migration to the
United States, the United Kingdom, Australia and New Zealand,
from countries such as Italy, Greece, Pakistan and the West
Indies.

It has been estimated by the Council of Europe that in order
to ease the situation sufficiently in that continent, at least
600 thousand people should leave it annually for a number of
years. In 1950 the Italian government announced that Italy had
a surplus population of three million and that a minimum of
450 thousand people would have to emigrate from that country
per year for a considerable time to come. About 65 thousand
leave Spain every year, and some 40 thousand the Netherlands.
Most other European countries have their own figures.[4]

Faced with the magnitude of this demographic problem, it is

not surprising that both the sending and the receiving countries should have set up a body to deal with it exclusively. The Inter-Governmental Committee for European Migration, representing 24 member nations, was created for this purpose in Europe in 1952. Since then it has assisted in the yearly movement overseas of an average of 120 thousand persons. Migration problems have also been attracting the attention of the International Labor Office, the population division of the United Nations organization, Unesco, and the Council of Europe. Finally, the problem is being tackled by many private demographic institutes such as the Research Group for Migration Problems and the European Center of Population Studies. These many agencies, as might naturally be expected, concentrate on the non-religious aspects of migration, particularly its economic and social, political and juridical, technical and psychological aspects.

Let us here take a look at the interrelation of race and immigration questions in the context of contemporary Britain, the United States and Australia. It is probably true to say that the years 1964 and 1965 have witnessed greater discussion of this matter in England than at any other period of its history.

Race and Immigration Control in Britain

It is often difficult to be sure whether the primary interest of this discussion is the immigration question or the race question as such. A book that appears to be dealing exclusively with the question of immigration will prove on examination to be also concerned with the question of race. Thus Elspeth Huxley has argued against allowing unrestricted immigration into Britain.[5] She seems to believe that there exists a somewhat mysterious "threshold" of numbers, a point up to which concentration of immigrants in any one place will be accepted, but that once this is exceeded trouble will result. For this reason she thinks that immigration into Britain has reached a point at which it is vitally important to apply drastic curbs. But she will not allow that her judgment is influenced by racial considerations. Indeed she is quite critical of those liberals who have attacked the Immigration Act of 1963 as a form of the color bar, whereas, according to her, it was aimed simply at limiting immigration in general.

The same Act has also been analyzed in terms of whether it was or was not adequate from the point of view of relating the flow of immigrants to the rate of absorption which the country could stand.[6] It was clearly to be inferred from the 1965 series of articles appearing in *The Times* of London that this rate was too slow at the present time and that the tide of immigration was even then too great for either the country's interests or those of the immigrants themselves.[7] What was not clear was what was meant by the country's capacity for absorbing immigrants. On the one hand, it could refer to the total number of people which the country could absorb in such a way that they would contribute more to the national economy than they would take out of it. But it could also mean the proportion of immigrants which the country could absorb without creating unbearable social frictions.

That the immigration question and the race question are inextricably intermixed has emerged indisputably from some recent political history.[8] One thinks, for example, of the case of Tom Stacey, who unsuccessfully fought North Hammersmith for the Conservatives in the 1964 general election and whose anti-immigration policy as outlined by himself[9] was based on the conviction that a nasty race problem in Britain "must grow rapidly unless immigration from the tropical world, where such fundamentally different attitudes towards life prevail among ordinary folk, is reduced to virtually nothing." Stacey claimed that throughout his campaign he found no immigrant who objected to his policy, but rather received "invariable support among the immigrants for the thesis that many more coming in would rouse hostility and would queer the pitch for those already here. 'The quickest way for Britain to destroy the Commonwealth,' I was told by a Ghanaian student of architecture living in Bolingbroke Road, 'will be for you to let in just so many that all this racial feeling breaks out into the open.' "

On the other hand, the Labor Party blamed the loss of their seats by Gordon Walker and Fenner Brockway on white antagonism to colored immigrants. It is believed to be the first time that the racial issue figured with any prominence in a British election. The Labor losses came in areas which have large colored populations, most of them Indians and Pakistanis. The race issue stemmed from the Labor Party's opposition in 1962 to the bill which restricted Commonwealth immigration into Britain. Although during the year prior to the elections Labor changed its mind and said that it now supported the measure, a "white backlash" struck at the Labor candidates at least in the Birmingham area.[10] Gordon Walker was defeated in Smethwick, an industrial suburb of Birmingham which had returned him to office since 1945. His Conservative opponent, on the other hand, schoolmaster Peter Griffiths, was successful on a platform of opposition to immigration.

British Labor and Conservative Attitudes

Since coming to power, the policy of the Labor Party in the matter of immigration has seemed to oscillate considerably. In February, 1965, the British home secretary, Sir Frank Soskice, told the House of Commons that immigration officers had been given the three-point mandate of submitting Commonwealth citizens seeking entry to an intensive grilling when necessary, imposing stricter conditions over periods of residence in Britain, and scrutinizing more clearly those who claim to be entitled to entry as dependents of immigrants.[11] Sir Frank said that in two years alone at least 10,000 immigrants had settled illegally in the country. "There is evidence," he said, "that, under existing control, evasion on a considerable scale is taking place. I cannot estimate at all closely how many have gained admission and

settled who should not, but I do not think their number during
the last two years can be less than 10,000. It is therefore necessary
to make stricter use of the existing powers of control, and for this
purpose fresh instructions are being issued to immigration
officers. We shall have to wait and see how effective these
measures are when in operation before deciding whether any
further steps are necessary." He added, however, that the government had already taken steps to initiate Commonwealth discussions to review the whole question of immigration.

In March, George Brown, economic secretary, gave a new
edge to the controversy by claiming that it was quite senseless to
talk about limiting immigration when Britain needed an expanding labor force. Speaking at Sheffield, he is reported as saying:
"It is absolutely mad at a time when our labor force is allegedly
overused and when our new labor force is going to rise only
slightly, that we should be talking about limiting the number of
people who can be used. It does not make any sense. This
country in the 1960's needs new people coming in to share in the
work as much as we ever needed it. Scratch any one of us and
you will find an immigrant not too far down. We have always
used them and that is the way in all periods of our history that
Britain has been able with a tiny population to do a disproportionate share of the world's trade." And then, introducing the
race issue, he went on: "If you have immigrants coming in, they
do not have to be black, white, brown or grey, or from across
the seas, or further up the island. If you have two people coming
in, that means two people wanting one house. Unless you build
more houses you create strain. I find in my constituency just the
same clash of feeling when a Scottish family or a Durham family
gets houses before the locals that you find somewhere else if a
Jamaican family gets housed."[12]

Yet in May a Labor Party spokesman announced that much
tighter controls and checks on the flow of immigrants—even
legal immigrants—into Britain were expected to be introduced

by the government during the Summer. It was accepted by all that such a move would represent a significant change in the Cabinet's thinking on the immigration issue. Going further, *The Sunday Times* for May 30 described it as a change of thinking on the part of the Cabinet "on color and immigration." Just how intermixed are the two questions, that of color and that of immigration, is shown by the fact that the same report went on immediately to say: "This new trend of thinking in the Labor Party means that the gap on the immigration issue between the two major parties is closing. Last week Sir Alec Douglas Home spelled out the Conservative approach to the color question: Immigration must be drastically reduced, until we can say that we are sure that the present numbers can be satisfactorily absorbed in our community life. If the government will not take the action required, we will do so."

Later, following the Commonwealth Prime Ministers' Conference in London in June, and the completion of the Mountbatten tour of Commonwealth countries and report on conditions and possible controls at the points of exit, the British government announced the most sweeping measure to date to restrict the flow of immigration into Britain. Limiting the number of immigrants from all countries other than Ireland to some 8,500 a year plus relatives, the new measure succeeded admirably in stemming the volume of colored immigration without too obviously leaving itself open to the charge of color prejudice. Of course it is obvious to everybody that the immigration problem has certain inevitable racial complications, and there are some, like the liberal Michael Foot, for whom (it seems to many) recognition of the problem and advocacy of any measures to keep it within bounds, is clearly and even blatantly racism.[13] Nevertheless, the 1965 restrictive measure, by not being confined to the limitation of Commonwealth immigrants only, gave the impression at least of being concerned specifically with immigration rather than with the color question.

Some statistics will show immediately how closely the immigration problem in Britain is allied to that of color or race. Until 1953 immigration constituted no problem at all from either the economic or the social point of view. Between 1947 and 1953, the balance was heavily in favor of emigration, the country sending out an annual average number of about 150,000 emigrants as against 65,000 immigrants coming in.[14] But from 1953 and especially 1955 on, the rate of immigration began to go up phenomenally, especially that of colored immigration. Up to 1955 there were in all only about 100,000 colored people resident in Britain. After that year, however, they increased at the rate of 35,000 annually until, in 1960, colored immigration reached the record level of nearly 60,000. In 1961 it had gone to the height of 125,000, some 50,000 of whom came from India and Pakistan.

The rate of West Indian immigration, in particular, increased fantastically. In 1948 this was a mere trickle of 547. By 1952 it had gone up to 1,293. In 1954 it reached the figure of 11,000, while by 1956 it was 30,000. Commenting on this the Eugenics Society of Britain said in 1958: "The enumeration is clearly imprecise, but it is evident that the total number of West Indians and other dark-skinned people in the United Kingdom at the present time is far greater than it has ever been before in the country's history and that the total of colored people—using that term in the loosest and most inclusive of senses—may approach 200,000."[15] And that was only 1958.

One of the reasons for the rapid increase of colored migration to Britain from the Commonwealth countries was the British Nationality Act of 1948. This Act, by creating the status of "citizen of the United Kingdom and Colonies," had conferred the rights of British citizens on people such as the West Indians, thereby opening the door for their migration to Britain. As early as April, 1958, the possibility that the United Kingdom might be forced by sheer weight of immigrant numbers into some kind of restrictive legislation was raised in the House of Commons.

The Pattern of British Immigration

But let us review British immigration legislation as a whole. During the Victorian era the entry and departure of aliens was regulated by no special laws.[16] The transition from the Victorian age to the twentieth century in this respect was marked by the Extradition Act of 1870, which made provision for the surrender of alien offenders to their own governments, and the Aliens Act of 1905, which provided for the weeding out of undesirable newcomers. These measures were inspired to a considerable degree by a fear of liberal and socialist ideology being brought in from the continent of Europe, especially after an upsurge of migration from Central and Eastern Europe.

But they were also inspired by the outlook of Tory members of Parliament such as Major William Evans Gordon of Stepney who, demanding immigration control in the name of race protectionism, had formed a militant racist organization called the "British Brothers' League."

Later Acts of 1914 and 1919 brought the system further development. Under these Acts, orders can be issued from time to time—for example the Aliens Order of 1953 or that of 1960—by which the admission of any alien may be refused at the discretion of the home secretary. As a result of these, the basic facts of the situation are that no alien may enter permanently without permission but that he may enter temporarily unless halted. The principle on which the measures were based is that Britain was not a country of immigration.

What caused the Commonwealth Immigration Act of 1963 to be put through was a realization that the existing measures were entirely inadequate.[17] The fact was that, since 1955, the United Kingdom had effectively become an immigration country for the first time in its history, especially for colored immigrants. And that it should do something about it seemed equally clear.

For one thing the old concept of the "Mother Country" had

begun to appear unrealistic, since there never had been unrestricted entry on an intra-Commonwealth basis. In any case it was clear that the idea of the "Mother Country" now held, at best, only for Australia, New Zealand and part of Canada. It was also felt that the United Kingdom could not contribute very much towards raising the standard of living in the colored Commonwealth countries through accepting immigration from them. Finally, there was the stark fact that, with normal natural increase, even the existing colored population of Britain would rise to enormous proportions by the end of the century.

This aspect of the matter was very evident in the utterances of Sir Cyril Osborne, leading protagonist of the 1963 Act, during the campaign for the introduction of the measure. In 1961, for example, the *Daily Mail* quoted him as saying: "This is a white man's country, and I want it to remain so." And in the *Spectator* during December, 1964, he said: "Those who so vehemently denounce the slogan 'Keep Britain White' should answer the question, do they want to turn it black? If unlimited immigration were allowed, we should ultimately become a chocolate-colored, Afro-Asian mixed society. That I do not want." Norman Pannell has calculated that the present colored population of 800,000 will rise to 1,250,000 by 1980. And if colored immigration were to continue at the rate of 50,000 a year, the figure for 1980 would be in the region of two million, and that for the end of the century, four million. This would represent some six percent of the total population of Britain as against about ten percent in the United States with all its race problems.

There were also, of course, other reasons for the Act. The housing and health problems were among these. The education problem also loomed large, leading to a situation of material segregation in certain places. For example, in Southall, with a high concentration of Indians and Pakistanis whose children frequented the local schools, English parents tended to move to other districts or transferred their children to other schools. Such developments were anything but desirable. Then, too, there was the popular belief that colored people are prone to certain grave offenses.[18]

Finally, there was the ever present fear of the effect of further immigration on the employment position. Thus Mr. Pannell has estimated that of the present 800,000 colored people in Britain, not more than 500,000 are usefully employed. In other words, they constitute only some two percent of the labor force. From this point of view, he has argued, they represent a dispensable element. This situation would be only intensified if British Railways, say, introduced more mechanization or lowered the retirement age of their employees. Even as things stand at present, there is always the danger of the appearance of material discrimination in the matter of the employment of colored people, either by relegating them to the under privileged jobs, or, if there is question of unemployment and redundancy, by laying them off more readily than British white workers.

The Commonwealth Immigration Act, 1963

These considerations help us to understand the background of the Commonwealth Immigration Act of 1963. Part I of this Act, Section 1, reads as follows:

> Subject to the following provisions of this section, an immigration officer may on the examination under this Part of the Act of any Commonwealth citizen to whom Section 1 of this Act applies who enters or seeks to enter the United Kingdom: a) refuse him admission into the United Kingdom; or b) admit him into the United Kingdom subject to a condition restricting the period for which he may remain there, with or without conditions for restricting his employment or occupation there.

Section 4 goes on to say that the immigration officer can refuse admission

> a) if it appears to the immigration officer on the advice of a medical inspector or, if no such inspector is available, of any

other duly qualified medical practitioner, that he is a person suffering from mental disorder, or that it is otherwise undesirable for medical reasons that he should be admitted; or b) if the immigration officer has reason to believe that he has been convicted in any country of any crime, wherever committed, which is an extradition crime within the meaning of the Extradition Acts, 1870–1935; or c) if his admission would, in the opinion of the Secretary of State, be contrary to the interests of national security.

This Act was heavily criticized from the outset as being both too loose and too tight in its provisions. Norman Pannell maintained that it was too loose.[19] Not, of course, that it did not have considerable effect in reducing immigration. For although nearly 95,000 colored immigrants "beat the gun," so to speak, before the Act came into operation, the fact that some 300,000 applicants were outstanding a year or two afterwards shows that it did cut down considerably the number of colored immigrants to the country. Nevertheless, writing early in 1965, Mr. Pannell argued that it still permitted many immigrants to enter the country under false pretenses as students, that it failed to compel genuine students to return home once their studies had been completed, and that it failed to make deportation applicable in the case of those people who are resident in the country for less than five years and whom it may have been found very desirable to repatriate.

Pleading for the introduction of a much more comprehensive control over the situation, Pannell demanded admission only on a selective basis on somewhat the same lines as that of the older Commonwealth countries, a general tightening up of the Act's regulations, and, in order to meet the problem fully, the introduction of further legislation discriminating "in the standards it imposed" so that the intending immigrant "should not become a charge on the public funds." There is no reference whatever here to the question of color, but one is forcibly reminded of similar standards—such as the "grandfather clause" or the literacy test—which in the United States have in the past provided masks, however poor, for legal measures that were racist in inspiration.

Almost diametrically opposite to Pannell's was the criticism of Cedric Thornberry that the provisions of the Commonwealth Immigration Act were too tight.[20] Mr. Thornberry lamented the failure of the Act to demand that the home secretary supply information concerning the grounds on which admission has been refused to an immigrant. The home secretary, operating within the provisions of the Aliens Act which enables him to vary the conditions for entry, etc., possesses boundless opportunity to create rules of law rather arbitrarily. Mr. Thornberry also complained of the failure of the Act to provide a means of appeal to a judicial or quasi-judicial tribunal which might review a rejected immigrant's application. As the Act stands, the application of the criteria of entry, even in the case of Commonwealth citizens, rests exclusively with the immigration officer.

Mr. Thornberry would like to see the Immigration Act reformed by the government's setting up a high-powered fact-finding committee which would take account of the technique of control elsewhere, by setting aliens and Commonwealth citizens on an equal footing, by clearly listing the various admissible categories as well as a list of grounds upon which persons can be refused permission to land or be naturalized, and by giving all immigrants a right to appeal by the creation of an "immigration and naturalization appeals tribunal."

Lord Brockway criticized the Act from an entirely different point of view. "Our complaint against the Commonwealth Immigration Act," he wrote, "is that it is racialist."[21] Other than on racist considerations, he argued, there is no case at all for immigration restriction. There is no danger at present of Britain becoming overpopulated. And if ever there should be, let the empty places of Canada, Australia and Africa relieve the problem by taking the surplus people. At present, on the contrary, transport, engineering and hospitals can be said to badly need the immigrants; in the future they may be a strain, but not now. Nor is there any danger of a lowering of wages through the employment of colored workers. For this would only be a serious threat if there were heavy unemployment and in areas in which immigrants were employed. Housing problems, too, are not insurmountable. Restriction of immigration is certainly not the way to solve this problem which, in any case, affects the indigenous as much as the immigrants.

Likewise Lord Brockway played down the difficulties arising in the fields of education and crime. Of the former he said that initial problems connected with the co-education of white and colored children can after a while be overcome, while as far as crime is concerned, the main problem—that of sex—diminishes considerably once immigrants' dependents begin to join them. There is also the fact that the pattern of conjugal relationships must be seen to be different in other areas of the world, particularly the West Indies.

The Times articles of January, 1965, while hinting at the need for some immigration control, drew attention to the fact that without the Commonwealth immigrants the health service would break down (some four percent of working doctors being from overseas, especially from India and Pakistan), the London Transport Service would be disrupted (over 3,000 Barbadians having been brought under special schemes to work for it alone), cafés badly hit, street cleaning made difficult of accomplishment, and Midlands industry slowed down.

It is against this background that Lord Brockway posed the question, "Have we the right to exclude?" and answered immediately and categorically, "No."[22] He would admit the principle that the government possesses the right to restrict immigration where necessary, but he would rigidly control its exercise of that right. In his own words:

> The right to control immigration numerically according to population pressure on the economy must be admitted, but not the right to determine the character of the immigration by race or color.

On the ground of employment, yes; on the ground of excessive population, yes; even on the ground of accommodation, yes; but on the ground of race or color, never. Once admit race as a factor, and one repudiates the basic principle of the integrated world and denies the human family; one accepts that there is some difference in personal quality between white, olive, yellow, brown and black, that the pigment of a person's skin decides the worth of his personality, that the physical is more important than the spiritual. In biblical terms this is the unforgivable sin, the sin against the Holy Ghost.

Lord Brockway admitted that many of the immigrants possess a different way of life from the British. But his attitude to this was that it calls for adjustment, by the provision of more and better social amenities, by the dispersal of immigrants as much as possible throughout the country, by the provision of liaison officers in immigrant areas, and by legislation against racial discrimination. Class bars and culture bars there may be, but a color bar should have no place in society.

It would seem true to say that in virtue of the race relations Act of 1965 and the immigration restriction Act of 1963 the government tried hopefully to have it both ways, seeming, at one and the same time, to be both opposed to racial discrimination and yet determined to restrict the entry of colored people into Britain. Later events (1968) were to hint that such hope may be vain, as witness the causes and effects of Enoch Powell's speech in April on the desirability of barring colored immigration almost entirely.

Immigration to the U.S.A.

Let us turn now to American immigration policy. Shortly before his death, President Kennedy wrote an interesting book on the subject under the title *A Nation of Immigrants*.[23] For that indeed is what the American people really is. Since 1607, when the first English settlers reached the New World, over 42,000,000 have migrated to what is now the United States—the largest migration of people in history. This migration was motivated by a variety of causes, religious persecution, political oppression, economic hardship. It went on in ever increasing proportions between the beginning of the seventeenth and the end of the nineteenth centuries. From the small figure of 150,000 in the 1820's, the number of foreign born living in the United States increased to 1.7 million in the 1840's, to 2.8 million in the 1870's, 5.2 million in the 1880's, and 8.8 million in the first decade of the twentieth century.

English, Irish, Germans and Italians were the predominant nationalities represented. The English came first during the seventeenth and eighteenth centuries. In the first half of the nineteenth century the Irish and Germans began to come, and the Italians by the end of the century. During this later period, too, Russians, Czechs, Hungarians, Poles, Rumanians, Greeks and Austrians began to find new homes and a new future in America. In fact between 1820 and 1963 the countries of Eastern and South Eastern Europe, including Italy, have sent over 15,000,000 immigrants to the United States.

Such a stream of immigration could scarcely be expected to take place without quickly creating tensions and problems. The undeniable poverty and crime on the part of some of the newcomers inevitably led to fear and hostility on the part of the earlier settlers. President Kennedy has quoted one New York newspaper complaining as follows about the advent of the Italians to the country: "The flood gates are open. The bars are down. The sally-ports are unguarded. The dam is washed away. The sewer is choked. . . . The scum of immigration is viscerating upon our shores. The horde of $9.60 steerage slime is being siphoned upon us from continental mud tanks."[24]

There was also some immigration from the Far East. This began in the latter part of the nineteenth century and was mainly to California and the West Coast. It was this immigration which led to the United States' first important immigration restriction, the Chinese Exclusion Act of 1882. This was introduced following on "nativist" agitation against the "yellow peril" and no further government action took place until after World War I. In 1917, however, the beginnings of a move towards further restriction could be discerned in the introduction of a literacy test for adult immigrants. Elements of racial discrimination could also be discerned in it. For it was undoubtedly intended to curb the numbers coming from South Eastern Europe.

In a way, this was highly understandable. In 1914, the high-water mark of American immigration, the country received a total of 1,218,480 immigrants. More than 800,000 of these had come from Italy, Russia and the Austro-Hungarian Empire. And over a quarter of a million of them were illiterates of fourteen years of age or over. But the racial element in the restrictions was kept in the background. While there was real alarm that many of the newcomers had little or no knowledge of the basic philosophy behind American institutions and ideals, fears as precise as this were rarely allowed expression. As in present-day England, the matter was veiled behind vague statements such as that of President Theodore Roosevelt to the effect that some limit would have to be placed to immigration unless America was to become "an international boardinghouse."

U.S. Immigration Legislation

In May, 1921, the Emergency Quota Act was brought into existence by President Harding's administration. By this measure the number of immigrants which any country could send to America in any given year was limited to three percent of the number of its people who were already in the United States in 1910. This law, however, was far from being a complete success. Many immigrants from the Eastern and Southern countries of Europe had come to the United States before 1910, and, therefore, these countries were entitled to large quotas. But there can be no doubt that the quota system had been intended to discriminate against them in favor of Britain, Ireland, Germany, Norway and Sweden and, in general, the Northern European countries.

And so a new law was passed in 1924, fixing the quota at two percent of the number of nationals of each country in the United States according to the census of 1890. The law also provided that after July, 1927, only about 150,000 immigrants would be admitted to the country each year. This number would be divided among the several countries in proportion to the numbers of their nationals already in the United States according to the census of 1920. The result of this was to put an effective stop to the flow of immigrants from certain countries. It also led to striking anomalies. For example, under the 1924 Act Ireland's quota was between 17,000 and 18,000 per annum. Of this it has used only an average of some 6,000. On the other hand, Italy's quota was between 5,000 and 6,000 per annum. This has been entirely inadequate to meet its needs—so inadequate, in fact, that the backlog of applicants for immigration from that country to the United States was no less than 132,000 in 1963. In the same year, the backlog for Greece was over 96,000, that country's annual quota being as low as 308.[25]

These various Immigration Acts were consolidated and continued by the Immigration and Nationality Act of 1952. Apart from some minor amendments and acts for special purposes (relating to the admission of refugees or the war brides which American soldiers had married in European countries), the provisions of the 1921 legislation—commonly known as the McCarron Act—have continued to dominate the situation.

Nevertheless, the United States has not fallen down badly in the matter of receiving immigrants.[26] Between the end of World War II and 1958, a total of 6.5 million people emigrated from Europe, mainly from Italy, Germany and the United Kingdom. Of these the United States received the largest number, 2.6 million immigrants in all. Still, in proportion to population, the United States ranks behind twelve others among the immigration countries of the world. Of course the population of the United States is itself undergoing a very rapid increase. At the end of

World War II it was in the region of 140,000,000; by 1958 it was over 171,000,000, and by 1975 it is estimated that it will be some 227,000,000. Nevertheless, in the post-war period, immigration into the country has accounted for less than 10 percent of its population increase and for less than one-fifth of one percent of its total population.

Apart from their racial bias and their favorable provisions relating to refugees and relatives, the American immigration laws may be said to be generally aimed at attracting skilled workers. But there are those who need help as well as those who can give it. As someone has put it so well, America cannot, as a nation, take only the strong and the brave, but must accept also its fair portion of the sick and the weak.

The general debate concerning the economic effects of immigration on a country is continual in America. The two ends of the argument always find support. There are those who re-echo the words of James Madison in the Constitutional Convention to the effect that "that part of America which has encouraged them [the immigrants] has advanced most rapidly in population, agriculture and the arts."[27] There are also those who repeat the sentiments expressed by a member of Congress in 1797. He argued that while a liberal immigration policy was fine while the country was relatively new and unsettled, now that America had reached its maturity and was, as he said, fully populated, immigration should stop.[28]

In 1963, Dr. Howard Rosen, manpower development officer of the United States Department of Labor, reported on some of the findings of the Department of Labor, which had attempted to evaluate the contribution of immigration in the past to the manpower resources of the country.[29] He insisted that conjecture about the likelihood of the immigrants contributing to unemployment is quite invalid because it is known with certainty that many of them brought skills that were badly needed.

On comparing the immigrants and the unemployed, he said,

one soon realizes that for the most part one is not talking about the same people. For one thing, the immigrants are in a different age grouping—25 to 44—the grouping, in fact, with the lowest unemployment rate in the labor force. Then again, one in three immigrants since 1947 has been in the professional, technical or skilled category, and therefore unlikely to be unemployed. Dr. Rosen continued: "It would be a tragic error if this country failed to fully recognize and appreciate the tremendous contribution that immigrants of different levels of education and skill can make to our society. In many cases these persons also bring with them a dynamic generating and stimulating force which always needs to be replenished in our economy."[30]

In January, 1965, President Johnson called on the United States Congress to rewrite the immigration laws and abolish the national origins quota system. "That system is incompatible with our basic American tradition," he declared in a letter to the House of Representatives and the Senate containing proposed amendments to the laws. While amending the quota system with a view to avoiding the anomalies it has created, the new proposals would not, however, substantially change the total number of immigrants allowed in each year. But it would mean that the total quota for each year would be likely to be filled and in this respect is very definitely a step in the right direction.[31]

Notes

1. Cf. G. Beijer, *Map Projecting the Spread of Refugees in Western Europe* (The Hague, 1952).

2. Cf. *International Migration, 1945–57* (International Labor Office, Geneva, 1959), pp. 57–61, 101, 109.

3. *Ibid.*

4. Cf. J. P. Schmitz, "General Trends in Migration from Europe," in *The International Migration Commission News*, April, 1954.

5. *Back Street, New Worlds* (London, 1965).

6. Cf. *The Times'* editorial, January 30, 1965.

7. "The Dark Million," January, 1965.

8. Cf. Nicholas Deakin (ed.), *Colour and The British Electorate* (London, 1965); Paul Foot, *Immigration and Race in British Politics* (London, 1965).

9. Cf. *The Sunday Times* (London), October 25, 1964.

10. Richard C. Longworth, "Britain's White Backlash," in *The Evening Press* (Dublin), October 16, 1964.

11. Cf. *Daily Mail*, February 5, 1965.

12. *The Sunday Times*, March 28, 1965.

13. Cf. *The Daily Telegraph*, Editorial, June 16, 1965.

14. Cf. Douglas Manley, "British Experience of Immigration," in *Migration News* (1956), No. 2.

15. G. C. L. Bestram, *West Indian Immigration* (London, 1958).

16. Cf. Cedric Thornberry, *The Stranger At the Gate: A Study of the Law on Aliens and Commonwealth Citizens* (London, 1964); Paul Foot, *op. cit.*

17. Cf. Norman Pannell and Fenner Brockway, *Immigration: What is the Answer?* (London, 1965).

18. This belief has been given some backing by books such as F. H. McClintock's *Crimes of Violence* (London, 1963), which has shown that the rate of colored crime is about six times as high as that of white, at least as regards certain offenses.

19. Pannell and Brockway, *op. cit.*, pp. 27–30.

20. Thornberry, *op. cit.*, p. 17.

21. Pannell and Brockway, *op. cit.*, p. 64.

22. *Ibid.*

23. New York, 1964.

24. *Op. cit.*, p. 58. Cf. also Daniel Lyons, S.J., "Immigration and the Golden Door," in *Christian Order*, V (1964), No. 9.

25. Cf. "American Immigration Policies and the International Scene," in *Migration News* (1958), No. 4.

26. Cf. *Ibid.*, p. 20.

27. Cited in Kennedy, *op. cit.*, p. 69.

28. *Ibid.*

29. "Manpower and Immigration in the United States," in *Migration News* (1963), No. 5.

30. *Ibid.*, p. 25.

31. Cf. Report in *The Irish Independent*, January 14, 1965; cf. als

Liam D. Bergin, "The U.S. Takes a New Look at Immigration," in *The Sunday Press*, April 25, 1965; M. A. Feighan, "Revision of the American Basic Immigration Law," in *Migration News* (1965), No. 4.

For Further Reading

M. T. Bennet, *American Immigration Policies*, Washington, 1963.

A. T. Bouscaren, *International Migrations Since 1945*, New York, 1963.

R. B. Davison, "West Indian Migration to Britain," in *The West Indian Economist*, IV (1961), 1–4.

Forgotten Issue—Our Immigration Policy, Philadelphia (American Friends Service Committee), 1965.

J. A. G. Griffith, "Legal Aspects of Immigration," in *Coloured Immigrants to Britain*, Oxford, 1960.

L. Grond, "The Influence of Immigration on the Demographic Growth of the United States," in *Migration News* (1964), No. 6.

"Immigration in Britain," in *Crucible* (Journal of the Church Assembly Board), London, (1965), No. 5.

Rudolf Klein, "Shame and Prejudice," in *The Observer*, 22 August, 1965.

Colin Legum, "Immigrants: U.K. Bid to Heal Breach", in *The Observer*, 3 March, 1968.

David Leitch, "The Race Rebels", in *The Sunday Times*, 26 September, 1965.

N. F. Maunder, "The New Jamaican Emigration," in *Social and Economic Studies*, IV (1965), No. 1.

Msgr. George Rochau, "Intra-European Migration in the Last Three Years," in *Migration News* (1965), No. 1.

David J. Shaw, "New United States Immigration Act," in *Migration News* (1958), No. 1.

Ivan Yates, "In Search of Enoch Powell," in *The Observer*, 28 April, 1968.

CHAPTER VIII

Race and Immigration: Australia

The close intermixture of the problems of race and migration is perhaps most evident in the policies of Australia.

Immigration and Post-War Australia

Clearly Australia has performed remarkable feats in the reception of immigrants. In 1962 the first secretary of the Department of Immigration was presented with the Nansen Medal, awarded to those making outstanding contributions to the solution of the refugee problems of Europe. By that year Australia had taken no less than 300,000 refugees since World War II, more in proportion to its population than any other country in the world. In all, since the war, there had been some 2,000,000 permanent arrivals in Australia, mainly British but many also from Southern and Eastern Europe.[1]

It is not at all surprising that Australia should be willing to open its doors to people from other lands. For Australia has been created precisely by the encouragement of immigration. During its early history, Edward Gibbon Wakefield produced his *Sketch for a Proposal for Colonising Australia*, a plan to bring out from England "young marriageable persons," men and women in equal numbers, in order to provide labor for the gentlemen already resident there. Indeed it was due to considerations such as this that, when the home country later found it desirable to transport convicts overseas, it was felt that, as Australia had been set up by England and given some preferential treatment in the past, it ought to be willing to put up with some discomfort for England's good by receiving at least some such immigrants.[2]

From a variety of points of view, immigration is of great importance to Australia. In 1956, the Right Honorable H. E. Holt, Australian minister for immigration, put the matter as follows:

> Security considerations place emphasis upon the need for the most rapid possible population increase. Economic considerations are not as clear-cut. They do lead to the conclusion, however, that there would be no short-term benefit from cutting the program. In the long term, opinion varies between: (a) the conclusion that continuation of the present level of immigration may mean, in the absence of increased overseas borrowing or investment, that there will have to be some higher level of internal saving (and lower level of consumption) than otherwise, but this will be a temporary phase which will lead to the creation of permanent assets and improved living standard; and (b) the conclusion that, in the absence of the present level of immigration, we might well have just as high a level of investment (and lower consumption) coupled with a higher average import propensity. In this case we would not have achieved the same population increase. . . . Whatever conclusion may be reached on the above issue, the simple fact is that immigration is one major influence that leaves the country with a long-term asset on both political and economic grounds.[3]

Similarly, Monsignor George Crennan, Australian representative on the International Catholic Migration Commission, has defended the view that immigration into Australia has been and is of tremendous advantage to the country's economic development. Since World War II especially, there has been a rapid program of development in Australia to which population growth, aided by immigration, has been of vital importance. Monsignor Crennan points out that in the iron and steel industry nearly half the work force came from overseas. In like manner, immigrants have provided much of the manpower for the development of the hydroelectric schemes, some 60 percent of the work force in one

case. The same is true in railway development; in one scheme
they provided up to 90 percent of the work force. Indeed it is
Monsignor Crennan's contention that if Australia can boast of
considerable post-war achievements—a stronger and more diver-
sified economy, increased productivity, spectacular increases in
living standards and dramatic advances in power, water supply,
railways, etc.—it is due in considerable degree to the contribution of immigrants.[4]

An Optimum Population Level for Australia?

It is on the basis of an analysis of these post-war developments
that Professor Colin Clark, Australian-born occupant of the
Chair of Agricultural Economics at Oxford, has declared that:
"the evidence appears fairly strong that rapid immigration is of
profound and lasting economic benefit to Australia, by enabling so
many Australian industries to enjoy the advantages of increasing
scale."[5]

In the opinion of many competent observers, immigration has
been and continues to be of such great importance to Australia
that it should be willing to receive new residents from almost
any source. This means that Australia should not be as biased as
heretofore in favor of British immigrants. To quote W. D.
Borrie, professor of demography at the Australian National
University:

> If Australia wishes to maintain immigration in the long term at
> recent levels—and I believe this should be the aim—we will have
> to be prepared to take immigrants from the sources from which
> they are available rather than from the sources which we might
> consider to be ideally suited to our own economy and culture.
> Australia, like Canada, New Zealand and Latin American
> countries, can no longer rely upon hand-picking the surplus
> population of Europe for immigrants, but must operate in com-
> petition with important magnets of immigration within Europe
> itself. . . . [Hence] while it is reasonable to take every step to
> increase the flow of British immigrants to levels that are com-

mensurate with the welfare both of the sending and receiving
countries, too much should not be expected from this source,
and to keep up our immigration targets we may have to continue
a liberal policy in terms of non-British settlers.[6]

Such sentiments cause many Australians to hesitate. There has
always been some hostility to immigration on the part of certain
classes, particularly the laboring class. From the 1890's on, this
attitude was fostered by the Labor Party and the trade unions,
who feared that immigration might lead to unemployment. Even
the British immigrant was only tolerated. The Italian immigrant,
however, was resisted, evidence that racial prejudice as well as
economic fear was part of the picture. At the present time, when
there is question of opening up Australia to a greater degree of
Asian immigration, this racial element has become more pronounced than ever before.

Professor Clark, for example, has argued that if Australia is to
attract immigrants, it must offer them a level of real wages that
is some 25 percent higher than that which they are capable of
receiving in their own countries. This means, he concludes, that
Australia will be unable to attract British immigrants at the rate
that is desirable. For the Australian manufacturer simply cannot
beat the British wage pattern and continue to export successfully
in the world's markets. For Clark the only result of Australia's
present policy will be to keep down the country's total population.
Based on these economic considerations, and making use of all
the available geographical knowledge about the areas of Australia
suitable for agricultural settlement, he places the ultimate population capacity of Australia at about 40,000,000. This figure is
given as a reasonable economic limit for a period as far ahead as
can be foreseen, but is not meant to be applicable for all time.[7]

Such predictions about Australia's population are not new. In
the 1920's, Griffith Taylor, professor of geography at the
University of Sydney, published a book in which he maintained
that the ultimate population capacity of the country was around

20,000,000.[8] Taylor's thesis was based on the idea that industrial development depended on the possession of resources such as coal and iron which Australia lacked. The view was keenly resented by the "big Australia" party and its author was forced to resign his Chair. On the other hand, in the 1930's, G. W. Thomson estimated that Australia could support up to 50,000,000 people, among whom the Chinese, the Japanese or other Asians would live at a far better standard than they were accustomed to in the countries of their birth.[9]

Whatever the possible final total or optimum population for Australia, it is generally agreed that the present increase, though considerable, is far from raising the specter of over-population. Even if at the end of this century Australia has attained a population of 25,000,000, its population density will still probably be among the lowest in the world, with a relatively small number of people covering some 3,000,000 square miles of territory.[10]

On Immigration Sunday, 1964, the Australian hierarchy issued a statement on the matter in the course of which they remarked that "the satisfaction derived from all that has been achieved in Australia's population growth and economic expansion needs to be tempered in the reflection that we still are a greatly under-populated and under-developed continent."

Pros and Cons of the "White Australia" Policy

The "White Australia" policy is the chief source of difficulty. There is no specific "White Australia" enactment, but contrary to what is generally believed, even by many Australians, Asians are excluded from the country if not by statutory decree, then by administrative action on the part of the minister for immigration. In virtue of an act which entitles him to impose a dictation test in any European language, he is empowered to exclude any person he chooses.[11]

This "particularly grotesque" clause in the act, as Colin Clark refers to it, has definitely resulted in discrimination against Asian immigrants. This in turn has raised a keen controversy concerning the 1,150,000 square miles of northern Australia that is known as the "Northern Territory." This area has been described as "a menace to the security of Australia, for it mockingly invites invasion from the teeming millions of aliens seeking expansion, less than a week's steam to the north."[12] The white man's attitude to the area has been simply to stand on guard "determined to defend, discuss and exploit the north. In fact, to do everything but go there."[13]

The reluctance of the white man to go north in Australia, both because it had originally been a convict settlement area and continues to be an area of low wages, has been a long-standing and well-established attitude. It was for this reason that during the nineteenth century, Robert Towns , a Sydney businessman, decided to import South Sea Islanders to work in his northern plantations. By 1868 there were over 2,000 of them in Queensland.

Despite an arrangement that when their contracts expired they would be sent back to their homes, the beginnings of a problem appeared in the increase of a half-caste population. Nevertheless, similar schemes to bring Chinese workers into the north were encouraged by the South Australian government after 1874. In 1876 negotiations were opened with the Japanese government to bring in farmers and peasant proprietors. These immigrants were to be afforded free passage and on arrival were to be free to settle in Australia. The arrangements were terminated by a revolt in Japan.

Very shortly, however, the Australian immigration policy began to tighten. Before the end of the century an act was passed in Queensland which compelled the Chinese to pay more gold mining fees than the whites. This was followed by a new and stricter bill which excluded aliens altogether from the goldfields. Likewise, in the Northern Territory, Port Darwin was closed entirely to Chinese immigrants. By 1901, the Chinese population had dwindled to about 30,000 and the "White Australia" policy had become firmly accepted by the federal government.

A contemporary Australian has written of this policy as follows: "The racial bitterness which attended the birth of the 'White Australia' policy has largely died away, but the fundamental object remains unaltered. It is, the average Australian declares stubbornly, not a racial or national discrimination, but an economic necessity. Its aim is 'to maintain the standard of living and the degree of civilization existing in Australia. Cheap labor of any kind which will tend to lower this standard is to be excluded.'"[14]

Colin Clark has examined the various arguments that are put up in favor of this "White Australia" policy. They include economic, political and medical arguments. The economic argument is already well known; it is centered in the maintenance of wages and living standards. But it is Clark's opinion that there is no point in wasting time over it, "for the basic assumption is not true."

The fact is, he points out, that colored immigrants who come to Australia get exactly the same wages as do whites. The only thing that would make a difference from this point of view would be the immigration of colored labor on an enormous scale and in such a way that they would have to be denied the civil and political rights of other Australians and compelled to work for lower wages. And so Professor Clark finds himself forced to the view that, although economic objections may be advanced against a program of large-scale admission of Asian immigrants, to say that economic considerations justify the rigid exclusion of all such immigrants is quite wrong. He says in fact: "We may be able to go on deceiving ourselves, but we will not deceive the rest of the world for long."[15]

He attributes greater force to the political and medical arguments. A policy of complete exclusion recommends itself easily to politicians, who are aware of what has happened in southern

United States where large white and colored populations find themselves compelled to try to live side by side. Indeed it was with this in mind that the Commonwealth government in 1907 not only excluded all further colored immigration into Australia but took steps to ensure the return to their homeland of all the Polynesian workers who had been brought in earlier to the Queensland sugar-cane fields. Likewise, in the 1920's, it was a standard argument of the Commonwealth government's medical advisers that a colored population would be the abundant carrier of diseases to which the native population had acquired considerable immunity.

Japan's Pressing Need of Emigration

Japan is the country which most frequently comes into the discussion of the Australian immigration policy. Even though birth control and abortion are widely practiced, demographers are of the opinion that Japan's population will continue to increase for at least several more decades.[16] It has been forecast, in fact, that it will go up to 107,000,000 by 1990, although some recession might be expected after the year 2000. What is morally certain at any rate is that Japan's population is likely to increase for another fifty years.

In addition to this, economists seem to agree that Japan is unlikely ever to become self-supporting in the matter of food. This is due to the poor agricultural base of the economy, the limited arable acres available being devoted mainly to the raising of starchy foods that can be consumed directly rather than to the production of livestock. This is one of the important factors in Japan's over-population problem. It would seem that the best that can be hoped for is that the present proportion of imported food, 20 percent, will not increase.[17]

Because of this situation, emigration is important for Japan. "There is but one healthy solution to the Japanese demographic problem," says a representative of that country, "and that is emigration. The effectiveness of this solution will depend mainly upon other nations' sense of international social justice."[18] Japanese emigration in the past has been considerable. They turned first, around 1885, to the Hawaiian Islands. Then, around 1898, they moved to California. After the restriction of these areas, first by the Gentleman's Agreement of 1907 and later by the National Quotas Law of 1924, they shifted their course to South America, especially Brazil. By 1940 some half-million Japanese were settled in South America, and the Pacific Islands.

But Asian countries also received their quotas. For the ten years preceding World War II, about 150,000 Japanese immigrants were annually received by Formosa, Korea and Manchuria. The Japanese defeat in World War II put an end to this. Indeed an opposite movement of repatriation took its place. About 3,000,000 Japanese living in Asia were forced to return home. In fact, between 1945 and 1957, some 6,250,000 of them were compelled to return home from overseas.[19]

During the post-war period emigration from Japan has virtually ceased. From the end of the war until June, 1957, only 16,796 persons were able to emigrate, of which 13,157 went to Brazil and 2,514 to Paraguay. Brazil's willingness to receive them may be due to Pope Pius XII's request that it open its doors to Japanese immigrants. Its spaces, he said, were vast and it should give special preference to Japan because this country had the greatest over-population problem of any nation.

The Brazilian authorities in responding to this made certain stipulations. They specified in particular that the immigrants must be experienced workers, must be financially assisted by their own government in the matter of equipment, and must settle exclusively in the tropical and sub-tropical areas which are not suitable for European colonists. Subject to these conditions, migration schemes have been negotiated between the Brazilian authorities and Japanese settler agencies.[20]

The possibility of Japanese immigration to United States

territory is also discussed. Some experts, such as the Dutch demographer Father Anthony Zimmerman, are quite optimistic that there is room and indeed need for it. In Father Zimmerman's words: "Plenty of land exists in the United States, which could theoretically serve the needs of the Japanese. In fact our surplus agriculture potential has become a source of embarrassment to the American economy."[21]

Alaska seems especially suitable.[22] With 586,400 square miles, it is twice the size of Texas and one-fifth of the total land extent of the United States. Yet its entire population numbers little more than 200,000. A contributor to the United States Year Book of Agriculture has explained that Alaska has been shunned by the white man because of the fear of the north which pervades Mediterranean culture; that it could reasonably expect a legitimate and vast growth of population; and that it could develop into a "greater Scandinavia": "There is little doubt . . . that if Alaska had been settled as long ago as Scandinavia by people of European culture it would now be supporting a larger population than Scandinavia and supporting it more easily."[23] If this be true, there can be no doubt but that Japanese farmers and fishermen could play an important part as immigrants in Alaska's development.

Should Australia Admit Asian Immigrants?

But it is to Australia that Japanese eyes are most frequently turned. And the big question for Australia in the matter of immigration policy is whether it should open its doors to migration from Asia and especially Japan. Despite his incisive criticism of this policy from certain points of view, Colin Clark has serious reservations about an affirmative answer:

> It is sometimes contended, both in Asia and elsewhere, that the teeming millions of Asia (revolting cliché) have some sort of right to settle in Australia, because it is one of the world's largest unpopulated areas, and lies comparatively close to them. This

reasoning is fallacious throughout. Many of its proponents are unaware of how little habitable much of Australia's area is. . . . The amount of land still available for agricultural development in Australia, though large in comparison with Australia's present agricultural area, is very small if measured on a world scale. If one really were in a position to redistribute the world's population from densely populated to under-populated areas, most of the move would be into Africa and Latin America, where huge areas of good potential agricultural land are still hardly developed at all. Australia would be of very minor importance in comparison with these continents.[24]

Clark points out that much of Asia is geographically nearer to Central Africa than it is to Australia. In addition, he asks what reason there is why those Asians who need to emigrate should not seek to go to developable land in Burma, Ceylon, much of Malaya and Indonesia, and there do the pioneering work themselves. He concludes:

According to the customary law and usage of nations it does not therefore appear that any Asian country can claim a right to send settlers to Australia. It is also generally accepted that Australia, like every other country, has the right to decide, absolutely, what sort of immigrant she is willing to accept, so long as she fulfills the moral obligation, less precisely defined, but binding upon her in the long run, to make the most rapid possible development of her economic resources, for the benefit of the rest of the world as well as herself. Australia therefore possesses this right, and she uses it, not, as is mistakenly claimed, on economic grounds, but on social, cultural and religious grounds. The formation of groups of settlers who differed, permanently, from their fellow citizens in these important respects, would not, in the long run, be conducive to social order. This is a sensible position on which the Australian's conscience can be clear, and which he should be able to defend against any international critic.

The only qualification which he would add—and it is an important one—is that "while an Australian statesman has both the right and the duty to act in this way, it is very doubtful whether he should apply the principle with such rigidity as it is applied at present."[25]

The cultural difficulty against unregulated immigration is a serious one. Despite certain national differences, it poses little problem in the case of a majority of Europeans. Italians have tended to settle in agriculture, the Dutch in the steel industry and the Germans generally in the cities. Of course the cultural pattern of Australia has undeniably undergone a considerable change due to the influence of immigration since the war. Hungarian influence has been noticed in music, Ukranian and Polish influence in painting, while the customs of many countries are reflected in folk dances and songs, in hair styles and even the cut of clothes.[26]

But cultural conflict has been reduced to a minimum due to steps to avoid personal and family disorganization among both first and second generation migrants to Australia. Measures taken or recommended to this end include the encouraging of immigrants to learn the English language as soon as possible, to marry and establish a family as soon as possible, and also to join national Australian cultural and social organizations.[27]

This does not mean that the wave of European immigration has caused no problems at all in Australia. There are some Australians who see the contemporary problem of crime in the country as due mainly to the careless admission of undesirable types from Southern Europe and especially Italy. And a non-Australian, John Cusack of the United States Bureau of Narcotics, has warned his own people concerning the "menace of Australian Mafia-type secret societies."

These notions may not be due to xenophobia, but they certainly do not correspond to the facts. Australian sources have pointed out that the highest rate of crime exists among the native born and the British immigrants. They report, too, that quite a number of the crimes of violence committed by young Latins during the past decade have been due, not to any inherent proneness in their temperament to violent and particularly erotic eruptions, but simply to the situation created by an imbalance of the sexes in the Australian immigration intake.

In 1962, a study by the Immigration Reform Group attempted to estimate the possible effects of lifting the present restrictions on non-European immigration to Australia in the light of experience of population movements in Africa, South Asia and Latin America.[28] Multi-racial societies and their problems were also examined, in particular, Hawaii, Brazil, Fiji, Malaya, Indonesia and East Africa, as well as the impact of Chinese immigrants on the communities in which they have settled and the "Negro question" in the United States. The study's carefully weighed conclusion is that a change in the Australian system of controlled migration so as to eliminate its racialist character could be designed without necessarily running any risk of the kind of serious conflict which has occurred in the other lands examined.

And yet there is need for caution. For if downward acculturation is an undesirable thing and to be avoided as much as possible, there are also problems in the opposite direction. It has been pointed out, for example, that "there are Chinese in America who consider themselves completely Americanized, speak English perfectly, know no Chinese, have adopted American nationality and the American way of life in its entirety, but that to conclude from this that these Chinese are fundamentally of the same culture as the Americans whose ancestors came from the Christian countries of Europe . . . is scarcely a legitimate conclusion from the premises."[29] Wherever situations like this prevail, there are bound to be at least hidden problems. One must remember too the possible implications of Pandit Nehru's opinion concerning what Australia might do to solve the problems of Asian over-population: "You would have to think in terms of millions, scores of millions, to make any difference."[30]

And yet for the past few years the conscience of the nation has

been aroused against the policy which admits some 100,000 to
125,000 British and European immigrants per year but closes the
door against the colored Asian. The Immigration Reform Association, formed in 1961 and active in six States, has been urging
a more flexible approach.[31] The association's arguments echo
much of what the Australian bishops and the apostolic delegate
have been saying about the matter. This is, firstly, that the color
bar is immoral; secondly, that Australia needs contacts with its
Asian neighbors; thirdly, that non-European immigration can
benefit the country, provided it is regulated according to
Australia's economic needs and cultural patterns; and fourthly,
that Australia's racial discrimination in the matter of immigration
has had a disastrous effect on non-European world opinion.

A rather pointed reference to Australia's problem was made in
1956 by the then apostolic delegate, Archbishop Romolo Carboni.
Speaking at a public reception on the occasion of a visit to the
north-western dioceses of Australia, he said: "It is far too
dangerous for Australia to keep the Territory empty and it would
be to your advantage to open the country here to big agricultural
and secondary industries and so invite trade with your nearer
Asian neighbors. It is better to keep healthy relations with these
countries than to ignore them."[32]

Similar views have been expressed from the empirical point
of view in a study by J. MacDonald Holmes.[33] This study, which
represents a geographer's comprehensive vision of Australia's
North, defends the view that the structure of the Territory is now
an anachronism which needs revising and forecasts that the
northern section of it will conduct its business directly with the
East more and more in the future. For since the war, and with
the development of modern communications, an entirely new
"problem of propinquity" between northern Australia and the
neighboring lands of Asia has emerged.

Still, as late as 1964, applications for members of Ceylonese
Burgher families to enter Australia were rejected by the Depart-

ment of Immigration. The department stated that its action was taken after its officers had studied the merits of the applications and had made necessary inquiries, but it declined to give any reason for its refusal to admit the applicants. It may be presumed, however, that the department did have good reasons, since already some 10,000 Ceylonese Burghers have been admitted to Australia, mostly since World War II. Nevertheless, the action was severely criticized.[34]

Socio-Economic Composition of the Australian Immigration Intake

Apart from the overall problem and the particular problem of the Northern Territory, there are certain subordinate problems in the pattern of Australian immigration. One of these is its apparent bias against agricultural immigrants. In Australia—possibly even more so than in other countries—the building up of industry has robbed agriculture of much of its labor force. In fact the present composition of the labor force, just 13 percent agricultural, gives Australia one of the lowest proportions in the world.

The immigration intake has been tailored to suit the industrial labor pool. Between the end of World War II and 1951, for example, some 170,000 displaced persons were brought from Europe to Australia on the promise that they would give two years' labor there wherever it was most needed. This meant that they were directed mainly towards the cities.

Urban bias. Australia's tastes are predominantly urban. There is no hierarchy of cities of varying size, or of moderately sized towns for that matter. Rather a sharp distinction exists between the metropolitan area and the rest of the country. Because of this, very many of the inhabitants of the smaller towns and the countryside look for opportunities to live in the city. This has led to the growth of a belief in the superiority of metropolitan over rural life, a belief which is encouraged by political, social and intellectual leaders. As Colin Clark has put it, it is now generally assumed in Australia that any man with any ability should go into industry if he gets the opportunity.[35] However much this attitude may be justified subjectively, it can and has led to discrimination by the authorities against many immigrants who might have wished to settle in the rural areas. This is a situation that is undesirable in itself.[36]

The settlement of migrants on the land could avoid cuts in immigration introduced on the ground that the country cannot afford a high standard of consumption and the capital outlay necessary to settle migrants.[37] Settlement on the land would also provide the kind of compromise that might well be welcomed by people who are unable to make a choice between the future benefits of a larger population and the immediate attractions of a high standard of living.

Normally, when a population is being increased by the intake of immigrants there is an increased demand for houses and services such as roads, water supply, sewerage and electricity. The money that is to provide housing materials, services, industrial opportunities, and so forth, must come from public loans, taxation, or the profits of industry that are not distributed in wages and dividends. The Australian public has left itself open to the charge that it is unwilling to provide the money necessary for absorbing immigrants because it prefers to have it spent on immediate enjoyment. But the problem can be avoided by the intake of immigrants who are willing to go on the land in a pioneering spirit. Some small communities of immigrants could be settled on the land as small scale, self-supporting farmers. Such land settlement of immigrant communities could be made at very little expense to the Australian taxpayer and with great advantage to the people brought in.

Imbalance of Sexes. A more significant problem in the pattern of Australian immigration is caused by the imbalance of the sexes among the immigrants, which seriously affects their social integration. In the years immediately after World War II the migration intake contained a considerable preponderance of men. Thus in the three years 1948–1950, of 409,000 immigrants into the country there were 62,000 more males than females. That this imbalance stems at least partially from the Australian immigration policy seems clear from the fact that, during the years 1957–1959, of an intake of 305,000, males exceeded females by fewer than 4,000 as a result of the government's efforts to increase the proportion of females.

Monsignor Crennan has argued that it is doubtful if a final solution can ever be reached. His reasons for thinking so are, firstly, that it is a demographic fact that at birth males exceed females by 5 percent; that since 1788 there has always been a surplus of males in Australia; that single females as compared with males are reluctant to migrate, and that there will always be many males who make the decision to remain in Australia after having come there first with the intention of remaining only temporarily.[38]

It is a curious thing that, side by side with this surplus of males, the proportion of women of each generation who remain unmarried in Australia has always been in the region of 10 percent to 14 percent.[39] Whatever of this, for Australia to discriminate against female immigration would be to give evidence of a very short-lived historical memory. In Australia's past the need to bring women in was a big one. Indeed the introduction of women settlers into a population hitherto overwhelmingly male (there were more than three males for every female in 1830) has been described as a critical factor in the growth and settlement of population in the Australia of the 1840's.[40] Many of these women were brought in thanks to the work of a great Australian, Caroline Chisholm, who also worked for the repatriation of children from English workhouses to Australia whither their parents had already migrated.

As far as the present is concerned, it should be remembered that the Australian State which has achieved the most rapid build-up of migrant population since 1947, is that State in which opportunities for female employment were greatest. Nor should it be forgotten that the trend in Australia has been for the marriage rate to fall, and that, by maintaining an increasing demand for a wide variety of goods, family migration and a sexual balance in migration to ensure an increasing potential marriage rate provide a powerful impetus for sustained growth in the economy.[41]

Notes

1. Cf. Kylie Tennant, *Australia: Her Story* (London, 1964), p. 269.
2. Cf. *ibid.*, p. 160.
3. "What Immigration Means to Australia," in *Migration News* (1957), No. 1, p. 20.
4. "Immigration as an Essential Element in the Economic and Social Development of Australia," in *Migration News* (1964), No. 3.
5. *Australia's Hopes and Fears* (London, 1955), p. 249.
6. *British People for the Commonwealth.* Cited in "Australia and the Future Flow of British Immigrants," in *Migration News* (1958), No. 2.
7. Clark, *op. cit.*, pp. 70–71.
8. Cited in *ibid.*, p. 62.
9. *Danger Spots in World Population* (Oxford, Ohio, 1930).
10. G. M. Crennan, "Australia and Migration," in *Migration News* (1961), No. 5, p. 3.
11. Clark, *op. cit.*, p. 44.
12. K. Tennant, *op. cit.*, p. 268.
13. *Ibid.*
14. *Ibid.*, p. 209.
15. *Op. cit.*, p. 48.
16. Cf. A. Zimmerman, *Overpopulation* (Washington, 1957), *passim.*
17. Cf. *ibid.*, pp. 20, 30 and 31.

18. H. E. Senzin Tsuruoka, "The Japanese Population Question: Reasons for Hope," in *Migration News* (1958), No. 4, p. 3.

19. *Loc. cit.*

20. Cf. "Post-War Japanese Migration," in *Migration News* (1957), No. 2; "Post-War Migration Problems in Japan," in *The International Labour Review*, January, 1957.

21. *Op. cit.*, p. 162.

22. Cf. George P. Carlin, "Free World Immigration, Demographic Trends and Japan," in *Migration News* (1958), No. 4.

23. Cited in *ibid.*

24. *Op. cit.*, pp. 50–51.

25. *Ibid.*, p. 52.

26. Cf. "The Influence of Migration on Australian Culture," in *Migration News* (1963), No. 4.

27. Cf. J. Zubrzycki, "Immigration and Cultural Conflict in Australia," in *Migration News* (1958), No. 1.

28. Kenneth Rivett (ed.), *Immigration Control or Colour Bar?* (Melbourne, 1962).

29. Most Rev. M. J. van Melckebeke, "The Chinese and the Problem of Conflicting Cultures," in *Migration News* (1963), No. 1.

30. Cited in Tennant, *op. cit.*, p. 279.

31. Cf. "White Australia Policy Questioned," in *The Advocate* (Melbourne), July 11, 1963.

32. Cf. "Empty Northern Territory a Danger to Australia: Apostolic Delegate's Warning at Darwin," in *The Advocate*, July 19, 1956.

33. *Australia's Open North* (Sydney, 1963).

34. Cf. *The Advocate*, August 6, 1964.

35. *Op. cit.*, p. 97.

36. Cf. "Les problèmes de l'établissement rural et de l'immigration," in *Documentation Catholique*, No. 1187, November 28, 1954.

37. Cf. "Land Settlement for Migrants," in *The Catholic Worker* (Melbourne), October, 1956.

38. In *Migration News* (1964), No. 3.

39. Cf. Clark, *op. cit.*, p. 55.

40. *Ibid.*, p. 34.

41. Cf. G. M. Crennan, "Immigration as an Essential Element in the Economic and Social Development of Australia," in *Migration News* (1964), No. 3.

For Further Reading

Australian Profile, Melbourne, 1960.

E. and B. Degrood, *Australia: New Home Country*, Utrecht, 1963.

A. R. Downer, *Australia and Asia: The Case for Our Immigration Policy*, Sydney, 1959.

Migrant Viewpoint on the Physical Development of Australia, Canberra, 1966.

K. Noma, *Population Explosion and Development of Underdeveloped Areas*, Institute of International Cooperation and Development, Tokyo, 1964.

N. Okuchi, "A Hundred Years of Japanese Migration," in *Migration News* (1965), No. 4.

C. A. Price, *Southern Europeans in Australia*, Melbourne, 1963.

—— (ed.), *The Study of Immigrants in Australia*, Canberra, 1960.

J. Mertens de Wilmers, "Warning Against Exaggerated Views on Overpopulation," in *Migration News* (1966), No. 1.

J. Zubrzycki, *Immigrants in Australia: A Demographic Survey*, Canberra, 1961.

CHAPTER IX

The Question of Miscegenation

Although seldom explicitedly admitted, the question of miscegenation or race mixture lies at the very heart of the problems with which we have been dealing. It is curious how people avoid facing this directly. Neither the segregationists nor the integrationists face up candidly to the relevance of the matter to the race issue. Among British writers on the subject, Cedric Thornberry seems to imply that the problems posed by the influx of colored people into Britain are primarily economic, while Fenner Brockway is ready to attribute the growing race prejudice in England to the influence of neo-Nazism with its idea of white superiority, to the bad example of anti-Semitism, to the propaganda of the British Ku Klux Klan—to anything, in fact, except a fear of miscegenation.[1]

Lord Brockway goes so far as to say in a simplistic manner that "the housing shortage is the main cause of racial bitterness."[2] At times, however, he does refer to the miscegenation fear. Thus, for example, when he says: "Sexual relations are the final test of race relations. I had begun to write that sex is probably the deepest reason for anti-color feeling, but on reflection I do not think this is true. When the question is asked whether one would like one's daughter to marry a colored man, the horror that idea arouses reflects not so much the cause of color prejudice as the result of color prejudice. It is due to the conception of colored persons as different and inferior. . . ."[3]

He is emphatic, however, that it would be quite unfair to class all who dislike mixed marriages as racialist, for one finds such among both white and colored who are otherwise friendly to each other. And he tries to deny the problem altogether by claiming that it is only a small minority of either colored or white persons who are maritally attracted to the other race.

Cedric Thornberry and Lord Brockway are against the color bar yet are slow to see a fear of race mixture as a reason for it. At the other end is Norman Pannell, who is in favor of restriction of colored immigration into Britain, but who is equally slow to assign a fear of miscegenation as a reason for this. Summarizing the situation as regards immigration and race in Britain, he says: "The chief difficulty arises from the great influx of unskilled colored workers of low social standards, of entirely different habits and background and possessing an imperfect knowledge of English."[4]

Sometimes he uses vague phrases that mask what otherwise might be an admission of the relevance of the miscegenation issue. Thus: "However heretical this may sound, it would clearly be wiser to accept temporary immigrants from the Continent than non-assimilable immigrants from the tropical Commonwealth."[5] That he has in mind difficulties in relation to miscegenation is clearly implied by Pannell when he says that "the fact has to be boldly faced that the only complete method of assimilation is by intermarriage with the indigenous population and absorption into the broad stream of British blood."[6]

He himself feels doubtful of the possibility of the success of such absorption as all significant previous examples of successful integration in Britain had been concerned with immigrants of the same ethnic group, because there is a form of self-segregation which resists absorption to be found among colored immigrants themselves, and because there is also a deep-seated unwillingness on the part of the white man.[7] But he is very slow to call it a fear of miscegenation.

The Deep-Seated Fear of Race Mixing

Why should miscegenation raise fears? The answer is that it raises fears because people are anything but certain as to what the effects of widespread race mixture would be. Suspicion of miscegenation is not new and it is shared by people of all races and nations. In the nineteenth century, before the Civil War, Louisiana forbade marriage between colored persons, even when freed from slavery, and white persons. Even today, although the U.S. Supreme Court has recently ruled in favor of an interracial marriage, marriage between whites and negroes is immediately legal in only 31 states.[8]

In Ethiopia, under Mussolini in 1937, even extra-marital sex relations between blacks and whites were forbidden. Similarly, in Germany at the Nuremberg Party Congress of 1935, a law was passed which forbade marriage and sexual relationships between Jews and Aryans.[9] The English until recently have been more tolerant towards miscegenation. In India, until about 1850, they had no great objection to intermarriage. Fears of miscegenation and accompanying policies of segregation are of comparatively recent origin in Britain. But that they are now there can scarcely be denied, and it is from them that Australia has adopted its attitude on race.[10]

Non-Europeans have their own opposition to the idea of miscegenation and their own reluctance to accept complete racial integration. Hindus, for example, simply will not mix; their religion and customs forbid intermarriage. And the anthropologist Raymond Firth has noted that in New Zealand, due to the social position of the Maori, the offspring of mixed marriages tend on the whole to retain and even stress their connection with the Maori group rather than to seek complete absorption in the European, although it is legally possible to do so and socially has precedent accorded to it.[11]

However this may be, that fear of miscegenation is a fundamental and even the most basic factor in the erection of racial barriers is a possibility that it would be foolish to ignore. Systems of segregation are born of the refusal to accept the implications of total integration which, in practice as well as in the domain of logic, is bound to lead to intermarriage and cross-breeding.

Speaking of the situation in Southern Rhodesia, one commentator has remarked that the whole policy of geographical segregation in that country presupposes the independent maintenance of the two races and the avoidance of a mixed race.[12] It is for this reason that social intercourse between them is not encouraged. For the miscegenation consequent upon full social integration and the fraternization between the sexes that must be part of it is certainly not something that will affect only the few. At the beginning perhaps, but consequent on the gradual increase in the number of mixed marriages and the accompanying break-down of social sanctions, a point will be reached where little opposition to such intermarriage remains and with little encouragement the process could engulf a whole population in a relatively short time.

Some testimonies will be of interest at this point. Writing about Rhodesia, the white settler Richard Haw says:

> One of the great fears of social integration is that it may lead to miscegenation. This fear drives many whites to extremes, and is used as a political stick to beat a shuddering electorate. . . . Racial crossing . . . is concurrently held in check by the mores of both Bantu and whites. These inhibitions would . . . surely be changed if social integration were facilitated. The consequences are undesirable in the present setting in Southern Africa. Apart from the fact that social mixing would encourage miscegenation, there is the fact that . . . racial tensions are thereby needlessly aroused. . . . To encourage different culture groups and races to live together is sociologically unsound.[13]

Similarly, Colin Clark has written concerning the relevance of miscegenation to the Australian policy of racial discrimination in the matter of immigration:

This is the crux of the question. The origin of racial discrimination, as has been pointed out by some shrewd historians in the United States, lies in the prohibition or discouragement of intermarriage. For, if you wish to prevent intermarriage, you will find that you will soon have to take steps to prevent whites and colored people from meeting socially. Even the strangest and apparently most indefensible restrictions, such as having different places in a bus for white and colored travelers, arise, basically, from this objective of preventing intermarriage. Those who object to such restrictions are obliging themselves, implicitly, to accept intermarriage.[14]

In a study on race mixture, prepared for Unesco in 1953, H. L. Shapiro has tried to explain the subjective reasons for this opposition to race mixture.[15] He finds it frequently associated with a high degree of development of racial consciousness on the part of the people who experience the fear in question. There is the fact, too, that the children of racial intermarriage find it very difficult to become properly integrated in society. They are either too small in numbers and therefore are taken under the wing of one or other of their parental groups, or, when large in number, they are often somewhat thinly distributed in society and as a result not easily integrated either. These children also experience difficulties which stem from the way their parental groups tend to think about each other respectively. Lastly, there is the role of imperialism in the past in framing the characteristic attitudes towards the question of race mixture.

Let us turn, however, to the objective reasons for miscegenation fears. Some people refuse to believe that any such objective reasons can be found. Pierre Cabanais, for example, maintained that the mixing of the races was the surest way of improving human nature.[16] Hitler, on the other hand, believed that crossbreeds are either weaker or more futile than animals of pure race. And Rosenberg held that they are culturally inferior. Like Gobineau and Chamberlain, he believed that the decline of cultures and the fall of empires is due solely to racial cross-

breeding.[17] Hence the National Socialist policy for the prevention
of the hybridization of the Aryan race especially through mixing
with the much inferior Jews.[18]

The Effects of Race Mixing

Biological. The effects of race mixture can be studied from the
point of view of biology, psychology and sociology. That race
mixture results in any deleterious biological effects was firmly
rejected by two of the earliest studies of the matter by the anthropologists Friedrich Retzel and Felix von Luschan.[19] A more
comprehensive study of the effects of race-crossing in Jamaica
was published by Charles B. Davenport and Morris Steggerda in
1929.[20] The results of this study were decisively anti-miscegena-
tion. The investigators maintained the general inferiority of
browns, that is hybrids, in stature and weight, and the presence
of physical disharmonies—for example, relatively short arms—on
the part of some of them. These results, however, have since
been questioned. In particular, it is not clear whether the
samples on which they were based were drawn from the
same age categories or stations in life in the case of each
group.

More recently, H. L. Shapiro has concluded on the basis of
a survey of existing studies that there is no reliable documentation to prove that race mixture as a biological process is inevitably
an injurious one.[21] He himself has studied the question in the
context of the Pitcairn Islanders, a small group of Polynesian-
English of completely mixed blood descended from the Bounty
Mutineers and Tahitian women. These provide a most interesting sample for the purposes in question, both because of their
complete separation from all other societies and because there is
no social prejudice among them. Shapiro found the physical
condition of these islanders excellent. Their height, in fact, was
almost an inch above the parental average, which might indicate

a vigor comparable to that known to result in the case of a large number of animal and plant crosses; the rude energy of the mongrel is proverbial.

Finally, there are the results of an inquiry held by scientists under the auspices of Unesco in 1951. A joint statement at this meeting by physical anthropologists declared that "as there is no reliable evidence that disadvantageous effects are produced thereby, no biological justification exists for prohibiting inter-marriage between persons of different races."[22] In a sense, this conclusion was only to be expected, for it seems eminently likely that the biological results of race fusion can scarcely be disastrous due to the essentially dynamic character of race.

Psychological. On the psychological side one of the earliest and most famous studies of the effects of race crossing has been Professor Eugen Fischer's investigation of the offspring of Boers and Hottentots in German South Africa.[23] He undertook this specifically with the intention of finding out whether they were intellectually and morally degenerate as had been maintained by some. While his findings did not allow him to confirm this, he did find his subjects utterly lacking in energy and a steady will. However, he admitted that this may be a social habit rather than a racial factor.

Davenport and Steggerda, for their part, came to the con-clusion that while blacks might be inferior to whites in planning and judgment but superior to them at music, the browns are inferior to blacks and whites in both respects. This is in line with their general thesis of hybrid inferiority.

Shapiro is more cautious in his conclusion. He insists that, on the psychological side, the consequences of race mixture are rather more controversial than on the biological. He draws attention to the fact that, due to difficulties in the matter of testing, many authorities reject as unjustified the conclusion that races differ psychologically in any significant way. Results give at best only averages, and to concentrate over-much on these would be to run the risk of losing the individual in the statistical mean. Despite this, he avers that it would be rash to deny entirely the possibility that psychological differences exist between races. But he could find no sufficient evidence for classifying the offspring of racial intermarriage as psychologically (or morally) inferior in any respect. On the contrary, in the case of the Pitcairn Islanders, he found them an upright, virtuous, intelligent and attractive people.

What can safely be said is that the Davenport and Steggerda thesis concerning the inferiority of racial cross-breeds is very much open to question. As in the biological domain, the techniques used by these researchers have been severely criticized on the grounds that extrinsic factors may not have been adequately eliminated. Other studies have shown that the hybrids are either intermediate in score between the whites and the Negroes, or that there is no relationship between the degree of intermixture and the test scores.

Cultural. The cultural effects of race mixture remain to be viewed. One contemporary writer has stated the position here particularly well: "The effects of race mixture are neither good nor bad in themselves; they depend on the quality of the individuals who have entered into the mixture, and on the manner in which the hybrid is accepted or treated by the community as a whole."[24] There seems to be little point in being opposed to miscegenation on grounds such as those defended by Professor Fischer, namely, that it always results in cultural decline. For over against this one finds the equally defensible view of Professor Friedrich Hertz, who points to the varied cultural attainments of the Jews, themselves the product of manifold crossings.

The question must be studied by way of the examination of concrete instances. One such is the mixed ethnical strain in Brazil, which has provided the basis for a new and relatively stable society. It has been government policy to obtain a mixture of ethnic groups in the new colonies so that "racial cysts" may be avoided as much as possible. And since the beginning of immigration into Brazil, the basic postulate has been the complete merging of the alien groups with the native Brazilians in order to endeavor to achieve a homogeneous society.[25] The result has been claimed by some to constitute valuable evidence of the high cultural level of a racially mixed society.

Some Qualified Conclusions

It is probable that some qualifications would need to be introduced, even if the basic contention in favor of miscegenation continues to be defended.

That the more general verdict is not against it is certain. Even the Eugenics Society of Britain has to grant that there is a certain amount to be said in favor of miscegenation. One of its published papers cites examples of cross-breeding between moderately similar, but still somewhat genetically and distinct, human groups which has led to the production of individuals and communities which have profited from that inter-mingling. Thus the Huguenot influx into the United Kingdom has been of special value to the resultant population in its inherent attributes.[26]

Elsewhere in the world, it points out, important examples of race mixture are to be found in South and Central America, where Spaniards and Portuguese, Negroes and indigenous people, have mingled in the last 300 years into a heterogeneous mass without excessive struggle. On a smaller scale Goa and Ceylon afford interesting examples of peaceful mixtures in the past of immigrant Europeans and dissimilar indigenous people. Among European nations France is given special mention for its receptivity and peaceful absorption of diverse immigrant streams. Attention is also drawn to the fact that Europeans and Eskimos have mingled almost completely to produce the West Greenlanders of today, while in New Zealand the process of Maori absorption has gone far.[27]

On the other hand, there are also examples of race mixing that have brought conflict and unhappiness in their train. For there are many factors, such as religion, aesthetics and ideologies, which can make wholesale racial mixture both highly unlikely and undesirable to many. The experience of Latin America, for example, has been pointed to as evidence of the fact that while large populations of varied descent can indeed live quite happily together, their cultural and economic achievements may be doubted. Colin Clark has suggested that in many parts of Latin America it would appear that the population of mixed descent has tended to remain at the rather simple cultural level of their colored ancestors rather than advance to the level of the white world. Indeed, he has gone so far as to say that some areas in Latin America now appear to be both culturally and economically worse off than they were in the seventeenth century.[28]

Ethical Aspects of the Question

In its most recent *Code of International Ethics*, the international Union of Social Studies at Malines proclaimed itself to be against miscegenation or at least opposed to the kind of emigration which results in racial fusion.[29] The reason which it gave for this was that "the differences between the various branches of the human race are so great that the fusion of races, though it always remains physiologically possible, is fraught with so many moral and social dangers that it is in no way desirable." It recommended that "fields for emigration should be opened up to members of different races on those continents which nature itself seems to have prepared for the different races. In this way harmful fusions could be avoided."

This Malines statement has been rejected by the Dutch demographer Father Zimmerman, who takes issue with it on the grounds that it is too sweeping. The fact is, he maintains, that all population movements are bound to result, sooner or later, in a real fusion between the original inhabitants and the newcomers. Racial fusion and migration go hand in hand. It is true that cultural intermingling cannot take place all at once. Time is needed for the development of a common consciousness and feeling of unity, through the possession of a common language, religion and customs. Sudden fusions have at times caused regrettable consequences. But natural processes can be successfully used to bring cultural contacts and fusions to a happier issue.[30] Father Zimmerman concludes:

> That mere biological racial fusion has evil biological effects we can simply deny. That biological fusion has evil moral and social effects by reason of genetical mixture, we likewise deny; by reason of social and cultural factors: we counterdistinguish. Ill-advised precipitate mingling of widely divergent cultures through intermarriage can have evil effects. Intermarriage between members of different races whose cultures have been integrated need have no evil moral and social effects at all. Natural selection of marriage partners, and mutual attraction or feelings of distance will play an important role in forming advantageous unions and avoiding those which are less desirable. No absolute rule can be given; attraction between some races is stronger than between others. . . .
>
> Is an immigration policy which restricts the influx of certain peoples because of the fear of moral and social dangers arising from inevitable racial fusion to be wholly condemned? If objective danger exists because ensuing fusions might be too precipitate, or might overwhelm the nation with divisive elements, a certain regulation might be necessary for the common welfare. This may take the form of selection of immigrants, direction of new immigrants to certain areas, laws designed toward integration, and possibly limitation of annual arrivals to reasonable quotas. Real social and moral dangers arising from immigration would appear to be an exception rather than the rule, however. One cannot overlook the possibility that immigration restrictions may be founded upon empty pretexts rather than upon objective reality.[31]

Notes

1. Cf. Cedric Thornberry, *The Stranger at the Gate* (London, 1964); Norman Pannell and Fenner Brockway, *Immigration: What is the Answer?* (London, 1965).
2. *Ibid.*, p. 79.
3. *Ibid.*, p. 84.
4. *Ibid.*, p. 47.
5. *Ibid.*, pp. 48–49.
6. *Ibid.*, p. 38.
7. *Ibid.*, p. 40.
8. The 19 states which prohibit interracial marriages are: Alabama, Arkansas, Delaware, Florida, North Carolina, Oklahoma, Georgia, Indiana, Kentucky, Louisiana, Maryland, Mississippi, Missouri, South Carolina, Tennessee, Texas, West Virginia, Virginia, and Wyoming. Cf. Albert I. Gordon, *Intermarriage* (Boston, 1964), Ch. 8, n. 7.
9. Cf. Irene Marinoff, *The Heresy of National Socialism* (London, 1941), p. 81.
10. According to Colin Clark, *Australian Hopes and Fears* (London, 1958), p. 50.
11. Cf. R. Firth, *Human Types: An Introduction to Social Anthropology* (New York, 1958), p. 28.
12. Cf. the official publication *The African in Southern Rhodesia*, in A. Richmond, *The Colour Problem* (London, 1955).
13. *No Other Home* (Bulawayo, 1961), cited in Patrick Keatley, *The Politics of Partnership* (London, 1963), p. 266.
14. *Op. cit.*, p. 49.
15. *Race Mixture* (Paris, 1953), pp. 23–28.
16. Cf. Jacques Barzun, *Race*, p. 59.
17. Cf. Marinoff, *op. cit.*, pp. 71–80.
18. *Ibid.*, p. 37.
19. Cf. Friedrich Hertz, *Race and Civilization* (London, 1928).
20. *Race Crossing in Jamaica* (Washington, 1929).
21. *Op. cit.*, pp. 50–52.
22. Cf. *The Race Concept* (Paris, 1952), p. 14.
23. *Die Rehobother Bastards und das Bastardierungsproblem beim Menschen* (Jena, 1913).
24. Otto Klineberg, *Race and Psychology* (Paris, Unesco, 5th Imp., 1958), p. 28.

25. Cf. *The Positive Contribution of Immigrants* (Paris, Unesco, 1955), pp. 145–147.
26. *West Indian Immigration* (London, 1958), p. 20.
27. *Ibid.*, p. 14.
28. Clark, *op. cit.*, p. 50.
29. Cf. *Code of International Ethics* (Westminster, 1953).
30. Cf. *Overpopulation* (Washington, 1957), pp. 177–182.
31. *Ibid.*, pp. 182–183.

For Further Reading

R. C. Adams, *Interracial Marriage in Hawaii*, New York, 1937.

W. E. Castle, "Biological and Social Consequences of Race Crossing," in *American Journal of Physical Anthropology*, IX (1926), 145–146.

————, "Race Mixture and Physical Disharmonies," in *Science*, LXXI (1930), 603–606.

C. B. Day, *A Study of Some Negro-White Families in the United States*, Harvard, 1932.

David M. Heer, "Negro-White Marriage in the United States," in *New Society*, August 26, 1965.

A. W. Lind, *An Island Community*, Chicago, 1938.

H. L. Sharpiro, *Descendants of the Mutineers of the Bounty*, Honolulu, 1929.

C. Wagley, *Race and Clan in Rural Brazil*, New York, 1952.

CHAPTER X

Race, Migration and the Gospel

While all aspects of the race question touch on matters of power and politics, it seems that power and politics alone cannot solve the problem. This is the considered opinion of experienced observers who see the real difficulty as consisting in a false concept of man which in turn is related to a false notion of God. One such observer is the Anglican priest, Trevor Huddleston, of South Africa. Racism in that country, he maintains, is the by-product of a theocracy that cannot be combated simply by catchwords about democracy. The racist must be fought and convicted on his own grounds. Writes Father Huddleston: "The doctrine of white supremacy is common to both Afrikaner and 'English' sections of the population. If it derives from the theological presuppositions of the Afrikaner and from the Calvinism which is their source, it derives equally from the failure of Anglicans, of Roman Catholics and of Methodists to live by the faith which they profess. To deny this is both dishonest and absurd."[1]

We find these sentiments re-echoed by the Reverend C. T. Wood, director of the South African Church Institute: "I hold that by far the most important factor in our approach to the vital problems that are confronting South Africa today is the theological one, that what really matters, that what really influences the Afrikaner, is what he thinks about God and God's purpose for him and his race. We make the greatest possible mistake in trying to fight his convictions with political weapons."[2]

Parallel views have been expressed in the United States by the director of the National Council of Churches' Commission on Religion and Race. "I think," writes Robert W. Spike, "that the explanation [of the race problem] is a failure of theological teaching and understanding. I do not mean that any specific heresy has been widely taught. In the main, a clear case against racism has been made by ministers, who have described it as sinful and abhorrent to God. But the congregations that listened to those declarations have continued to practice racism. This separation of preaching from practice—the belief that the gospel is some pure, unattainable ideal—is close to being the Protestant heresy."[3]

Christianity and Human Equality

Historical experience suggests that one of the most influential—and badly needed—social principles which derive from the gospel of Christianity is that of the human status and the equal status of all men. There is an evident tendency among men to consider their group alone as fully human. The habit of primitive peoples, such as the Zulus, of calling themselves "the people" and others "animals" is not without analogies among civilized peoples.

Thus it was that the Greeks and Romans distinguished themselves from what were known as "barbarians." In its original sense the term "barbarism" was not contemptuous; essentially it meant simply those people who made noises like "bar-bar" instead of talking Greek.[4] Not all such people were primitive or uncivilized and this the Greeks knew full well. Nevertheless, to the Greek way of thinking, the fact that they did not speak the Greek tongue meant that they did not live or think in a Greek way either. And for the Greeks this was a fact which made a great difference. For one thing, it meant that the barbarians did not live in city-states as did the Greeks. As a result they could not be described as "political animals." But Aristotle had defined man as a political animal, that is, one whose characteristic it was to live in a city-state. Hence it was that, willy-nilly, the Greeks were forced to regard the barbarians as something less than man at his best and most characteristic. Indeed they quickly came to look on them as inferior beings—fit material for the institution of slavery. For it was Greek institutions, and in particular the political and cultural institutions of the city-state, which, by ensuring respect for his rights and enriching his life in general, conferred on man what is known as "freedom." It was against this background that the Greeks formulated the axiom: "The barbarians are slaves; we Hellenes are free men."[5]

It is not surprising that Aristotle should have linked these ideas with his theory of natural slavery. In the *Nicomachean Ethics* he indicates clearly that his idea of the slave did not at all imply inferiority or inequality that is exclusively due to race. Rather is it that those men were by nature suited to slavery who knew not the "freedom" of the Greeks. And such, as a whole, were the barbarians who must therefore be classed as pertaining to a lesser grade of humanity. This was a conception that was adopted by the Romans, who in their turn glorified the characteristics embraced by *Romanitas* (Roman-ness).[6]

H. D. Kitto, in his book on the Greeks, takes the position that in thus distinguishing themselves sharply from all foreigners, who were regarded as inferior, the Greco-Romans were paralleled only by the Jews. There was this difference, however, that whereas the Greek conception of barbarian inferiority was not at all racial in its foundation, the Jewish conception of Jewish uniqueness was.[7] In virtue of their conviction that God had chosen them, they tended to see a great gulf between them and the gentiles, although rabbinic teaching always maintained that "the righteous of all peoples have their portion in the world to come" if they fulfill the seven commandments of the sons of Noah (cf. Gen 9:1–17). For the Jews it was not political or cultural institutions but possession of the law of God which gave men the freedom of the sons of God.

Arnold Toynbee has pointed out[8] that the Jewish division of mankind into superior and inferior, Jew and gentile, was reproduced once more (though in somewhat different form) by the Pauline dichotomy of "vessels of mercy prepared unto glory" and "vessels of wrath fitted to destruction" (Rom 9:22–23). The only difference is that it was the freedom of the law of Christ that now specified the sons of God, and that, in addition and most importantly, the dividing line was now drawn between individuals rather than between communities.

The principle of division, however, did not remain thus for long. By the middle ages we find mankind classified as "Christian" and "heathen" and, despite the fact that the heathens were not looked upon as either irretrievably cut off from, or incurably inferior to, the Christians, much was done in virtue of the distinction between them that smacks of modern racism.

It is Toynbee's contention that the mediaeval world was relatively free from the prejudice of race-feeling.[9] As he sees things, the emergence of modern race theories is a product of the "Bible Christian" mentality which identified Europe with Israel and non-Europeans with the Canaanites, a mentality which accompanied British conquest in the New World and, by a circuitous route, came back to Europe later to find new forms in the Nordic myth.[10] Even today there are still to be found biblical fundamentalists who claim to be "the chosen people." For example, in 1963 a British noblewoman wrote in an Irish newspaper:

If there is ever an earthquake, pestilence, famine or floods, the quickest and best rescue work is at once carried out by the English-speaking peoples. I am very keen that our brethren of the United States should now return to us and build up this mighty union. At the risk of being regarded as a religious crank, I wish to state that I entirely believe the ancient prophecies in the Bible and I believe we undoubtably are "the Covenant People" spoken of in the Bible and we are under a direct mission from the Almighty.[11]

Such perversions of the biblical message have led Toynbee to maintain that "all our modern Western 'race theories' are lineally descended" from "the Jewish and Christian theological system" (p. 245). However exaggerated this statement may be, it clearly reveals the extent to which the message of the Bible can be and has been deformed over the course of centuries to suit the interests of its professed adherents.

Christianity Has Always Opposed Racism

Officially, if not in all its members, the Christian church has been resolutely opposed to all race theories. Its attitude is based on a fundamental belief in the essential unity and equality of all men. This principle is a necessary part of its doctrine and is implied by its practice at all times. As far as Scripture and the teaching of the fathers of the church are concerned, race theories are entirely excluded by an insistence on the unity and dignity of all men. The unity of men springs from their common origin and common destiny. The fathers regarded the Genesis story as implying the unity of mankind; they also taught a unity of destiny for all. St. Paul's teaching on the universality of salvation is relevant here. Sin affected all, and so does the redemption of Christ. Indeed the unity of mankind will become most manifest, according to St. Paul, when all men have become one in Christ.

This basic human unity is compatible with the simultaneous emergence of multiple "human" branches from the one original primate stock. Admittedly the question of the nature of original sin in such conditions presents new difficulties, but that they are far from being entirely insurmountable has been shown clearly by theologians.[12] In other words, a polytypic concept of the human species would not necessarily contradict human unity. All would possess the same human nature, have the same needs and the same human dignity. That human dignity is the same for all is by no means an exclusively Christian attitude. It was recognized of old by the Stoic philosophers; Christianity simply gave it a practical recognition.

The attitude of Christianity to racism is perhaps most clearly to be discovered in the pattern of its missionary practice.[13] This provides clear evidence of a practical belief that there is no more a separate church for each race than there is a separate God for each. True, in practice and to a degree, Christianity admits the existence of "national" churches with somewhat different laws and forms of ritual. But this is merely a realistic acceptance of the sociological phenomenon of the variability of culture. From the time of St. Paul the church has always insisted that in the mystical body of Christ there is neither Jew nor Greek, neither bond nor free, neither male nor female. The very language used makes clear the meaning of St. Paul's message. For it was evident that there were both men and women in the church, indeed at that time both free men and slaves. What he meant to underline was the fundamental unity of all. Hence, though the Christian church does adapt itself to peoples and races, it cannot tolerate the idea of national churches in complete isolation from one another. Indeed adaptation in the church in the past and as outlined for the future by Paul VI's encyclical *Ecclesiam Suam* is itself something that is designed for the purpose of securing better unity and integration in the one and universal church of Christ.

In this connection one might note in particular the efforts of the Roman Catholic Church to create a native clergy. In the instructions of Propaganda Fide as early as 1630, in the encyclical *Maximum Illud* of Benedict XV in 1919, in the encyclical *Rerum Ecclesiae* of Pius XI in 1926, and in the encyclical *Evangelii Praecones* of Pius XII in 1951, considerable importance is attached to this effort. One might note too the action of Pope Pius XII at the outbreak of World War II in consecrating twelve missionary bishops from twelve different countries widely scattered over the globe.

Despite the unfortunate incident of the Chinese Rites, the fact is that the church wishes to adapt itself as much as possible to the different customs of peoples. For although there are no radically different races, there are different characteristics among peoples which must be taken into account. Indeed some Christian thinkers would go very far in this direction.[14]

The traditional teaching of Christian theologians has been generally opposed to anything like racism. No race prejudice as such can be discerned in the mediaeval troubles with the Jews, the wars against the Moors and Slavs, or the later crusades against Islam. All these were looked on and treated rather as "unbelievers."

This point is poorly understood. It means, in effect, that white-colored relations were viewed for centuries in terms of the progress of Christianity at the inevitable cost of the so-called "infidel" peoples. It was this attitude which was institutionalized by the jurists of the high middle ages, for example Hostiensis (*circa* 1271), who proclaimed that all infidels might be conquered in the interests of their conversion to Christianity.[15] In accordance with this we find Pope Nicholas V (1447–1455) issuing bulls to Henry the Navigator permitting him to seize slaves among the Moors and pagans in the pious hope that it would lead to their conversion.[16] We know only too well how these theological considerations were exploited by the *conquistadores* of the New World.

Why Did Christianity Once Permit Slavery?

There is one problem which raises some difficulties, although in truth they are more apparent than real. I refer, of course, to the question of slavery. That the Christian church allowed it at the beginning is undeniable. St. Paul's denial of the existence of bond and free in the church is as credible as is the absence of male and female. On the contrary his point was that both bond and free, male and female, were one in Christ Jesus, our Lord.

Elsewhere indeed he said explicitly that "whether bond or free" we are all the children of God.

It is quite probable that the tolerance of the early church towards the institution of slavery was motivated by a desire to show that Christianity was a religion of peace rather than of violence. Hence the church's urging that Christian slaves should obey their masters.[17]

Whatever the practice of the early church, the first serious blow to slavery was the church's attack on the teaching on which it was founded. Very quickly it became clear to Christians that the philosophical grounds for the Aristotelian theory of natural servitude were false and incompatible with Christian teaching. Gradually, too, the practice of slavery by Christians came to be dropped. The laws of successive Christian emperors gave greater possibilities of enfranchisement to slaves.[18] By the middle ages a considerable body of legislation censured Christians who reduced to servitude those emancipated within the enclosure of a church. In so far as the mediaeval church itself owned serfs, these resembled peasants rather than slaves.[19]

When eventually in 1435 Pope Eugenius IV issued a bull on slavery to the bishops of the Canary Islands, it was but the logical development of a long historical process. The pope wrote:

> As We have quite recently learned, certain Christians—a very painful thing to say—have invented divers pretexts and made occasions arise for landing upon the Isles with their ships and armed troops. They have brought away as slaves with them into other countries upon this side of the seas persons of both sexes. Now it belongs to Us, above all others, to correct every sinner for his sin. We beg the temporal princes and all the other faithful of Christ of no matter what state, to renounce the above-named acts and to cause their subjects to turn aside from them and to repress them severely. We order and command all and each of the faithful to restore to their original freedom completely and forever and within fifteen days from the publication of this Bull to allow to depart without exaction of money payment all the inhabitants of the said Isles whom they have made captive.[20]

Similar condemnations of slavery were issued by Popes Pius II in 1462, Paul III in 1537, Urban VIII in 1639, Benedict XIV in 1741, Pius VIII in 1815, Gregory XVI in 1839 and Leo XIII in 1888.

The attitude of the early church to slavery, therefore, provides no basis for the attribution of any racist ideas. Racist ideas as such seem to have first emerged in the sixteenth century with the beginning of the era of colonialism. Although as yet there were no race theories in the philosophical sense, race prejudice and antipathies began to be manifest, especially among certain Spaniards after the conquest of America. Some maintained that the Indians, even though they appeared to be so, were not men at all, the reason being that they had insufficient intelligence. Others held that even if they were in fact men, they were cut out to be what Aristotle had called "natural" slaves.[21]

As with so many other human institutions, such as the state and private property to mention but two, the fathers of the church had earlier come to accept the institution of slavery as something in harmony with the natural law. Not the primary law of nature, but the secondary, that is, as characteristic of man vitiated by the fall. In this same line of thought, St. Thomas regarded it as stemming from the law of nations, which represented the universal or quasi-universal practice of mankind in response to the urging of the secondary principles of natural law. In other words, he found it natural that slavery should exist, it being useful that the serfs—assumed to be of lesser intelligence— should be governed by wiser men.

The doctrine of utility, as thus expounded, found considerable favor among Spanish scholastics of the sixteenth century. Palacios Rubios, for example, saw slavery as a matter of international law governing the conduct of war. For whereas God created the human race free, the needs of war entail that the conquered should be the slaves of the victor, something confirmed everywhere by the law of nations. It was for similar reasons that the

Scotsman John Major could write in 1510 that the inhabitants of the New World "live like beasts [and that] therefore the first one to occupy those lands may in law rule over their inhabitants, for it is clear that they are by nature serfs."[22]

Aristotle vs. Christian Thought

But it was the non-scholastic Gines de Sepulveda who has become most notorious for the expression of such views. Sepulveda was more racist in tendency than any of his predecessors. It was he, in his book *Democrates Alter* written about 1547, who said: "These people are as inferior to the Spaniards as children are to adults and women to men; there is as great a difference between them as there is between savagery and forbearance, between violence and moderation, almost—I am inclined to say—between monkeys and men."[23] It has been maintained of course that the exact meaning of the Sepulvedan doctrine of natural servitude is not clear. According to some it was meant to be a defense of serfdom rather than of slavery in the strict sense of that term. Although this is possible it is unlikely in that were it so Sepulveda's teaching might reasonably be expected to have been understood by his contemporaries.[24]

It was precisely in response to a complaint by one of the Mexican bishops against the propagation of ideas such as these in the New World, that Pope Paul III in 1537 issued a series of bulls which represent the first specific Roman pronouncements on race questions. In these he insisted that the Indians were indeed men, that they must not be enslaved as if they were sub-human and that such action incurred the penalty of excommunication. The pope wrote:

> We know that this same Truth which can neither deceive nor be deceived, when it sent the Preachers of the Faith to perform this mission, said: 'Go forth and teach all men'; go to all men indiscriminately, for all are capable of receiving the teaching of our faith . . . these same Indians as true men . . . are capable of

receiving Christian faith. . . . We declare that these Indians and all other peoples who from now on may come to the notice of Christians, even though they may be outside the Christian faith, are not, and should not be, deprived of their freedom or of control over their possessions. . . . They should be attracted to, and persuaded to embrace, the Christian faith. . . . [25]

An important aspect of this argument as expounded by Pope Paul III is that it was not simply empirical. It did not examine the extent to which the Indians or any other people were endowed with reason, but was a general judgment concerning mankind as a whole. For this reason it was quickly applied in the case of Negroes as well as that of the Indians about whom it was originally issued.

The most famous writers who opposed racist concepts during the sixteenth century were the Dominican philosophers Francisco de Vitoria and Fra Bartholomew de Las Casas. What is generally accepted as the first important treatise on international law is Vitoria's defense of the Indians published in 1539. In this, his famous *De Indis*, he maintained that, as they were men, the natural law applied to them equally as it did to the Spaniards. In a similar vein, Las Casas wrote a treatise entitled *Apologetic History*, an anthropological work completed about 1547, in which the Indians were shown to be anything but semi-animals. In Las Casas' work the question of racism, slavery, war and conquest overlap in a way that does not at all make for clarity of exposition. Thus his rejection of racist ideas is particularly linked with a rejection of ideas about a natural servitude. Not that he rejected in itself the Aristotelian theory of natural servitude. What he did reject was that it should be arbitrarily applied to the Indians.

Even before Las Casas, certain other sixteenth-century Spanish writers, such as Bernardo de Mesa, had expressed surprise at the idea that there should be so many human beings who were irrational. This approach was effectively used by Las Casas to argue that the feebleminded among mankind must necessarily be very few and that the thesis about natural servitude could not legitimately be applied to whole peoples such as the Indians. Those suited for servitude, he said, are "like monsters among mankind, and such must be very few in number and seldom found." On the subject of the Indians he pressed his argument as follows: "It is thus impossible, even if we had not seen the country with our own eyes, that they could be serfs by nature and therefore monsters among mankind, since nature always works perfectly and does not err except in the very smallest degree."[26] To say anything else, Las Casas assumed, would be to accuse the Creator of a major error.

Modern writers sometimes express surprise at Las Casas' acceptance of the theory of natural slavery. One suggested explanation of this is that his purpose was not to attack Aristotle frontally, but rather to show that the doctrine was not applicable to the Indians. But Las Casas also moved on to the idea of the essential non-empirical unity of mankind, as is clear from the following passage: "All the nations of the world are men, and for each and all of them there is only one definition: all have understanding and will; all have five external senses and four internal, by which they are motivated; all rejoice in the good and have pleasure in what is delightful and joyful, and all reject and abhor evil and are hostile towards what is disagreeable and harmful."[27] In accordance with this he believed that all men can become civilized, a doctrine indicating a philosophical faith in human progress.

The years 1550 and 1551 were the occasion for a great debate at Valladolid concerning the application of the theory of natural slavery to the Indians. Although the outcome of this famous contest between Sepulveda and Las Casas continues to be disputed, it had the astonishing result of causing the Emperor Charles V to suspend further Spanish conquests in the New World until a decision of some kind had been reached.[28] In the light of this the popular image of an amoral Spanish colonialism in the sixteenth century could certainly do with some recasting.[29]

Just how relevant the Aristotelian theory of natural inferiority is to the contemporary race question can be estimated from the overtones of the following exposé of the ethics of segregation in the United States by Father William J. Kenealy, S.J.: "The fundamental principles of the natural law . . . are obviously incompatible with compulsory segregation unless: the Negro is not a man; or, if he is a man, then an essentially inferior man; or, if he is not an essentially inferior man, then an accidentally inferior man, whose accidental inferiorities unfit him, *as a Negro*, for free association with the allegedly superior white man."[30]

Hence it is that, once again in the middle of the twentieth century, the old problem raises its still vigorous head. It is of immense importance that Christians should be in the forefront of the struggle again. To fail in this would be to leave ourselves open to even more serious charges than those levelled by Hochhuth's play against Pope Pius XII in the matter of the defense of the Jews.

From Theory to Practice

In a publication prepared for Unesco, Father Yves Congar draws attention to a long series of pronouncements by popes and national Catholic hierarchies against the race theories of Nazism and Fascism.[31] These include a pastoral letter of the Bavarian episcopate (1931), a joint pastoral of the Austrian episcopate (1933), a joint pastoral of the German episcopate (1934), the encyclical letter of Pope Pius XI *Mit Brennender Sorge* (1937), a letter from the Sacred Congregation of Seminaries and Universities urging Catholic centers of learning to refute racism (1938), an address by Pope Pius XI to students of Propaganda Fide opposing race theories (1938), and four addresses—all in 1938— by Cardinals Faulhaber of Munich, Van Roey of Malines, Verdier of Paris and Schuster of Milan.

The letter from the Sacred Congregation of Seminaries and Universities (1938) was a kind of "syllabus of errors," though

contrasting considerably in purpose to its prototype. Students
were instructed to combat several propositions which were considered to be the logical conclusions of certain less blatant
popular notions. Among these condemned propositions were that
"the races of mankind, by their natural and immutable characteristics, differ so widely that the lowest among them is further from
the highest man than from the highest animal species," and that
"the essential aim of education is to develop the characteristics
of the race and to kindle in men's minds a burning love of their
own race as the supreme good."[32]

However, it is one thing to have moral obligations enunciated
by the institutional church; it is another for the Christian community to give them practical assent and implementation. One is
reminded of the clerical voices that were raised in vain against
the enforced slavery of Negroes in sixteenth-century Spanish
America. Friar Alonso de Montufar protested: "We do not
know what reason there may be for Negroes to be captives any
more than Indians for, according to what we hear, they willingly
receive the Holy Gospel and do not make war upon Christians,"
and Friars Bartolomé de Albornoz and Domingo de Soto
earnestly agreed.[33] But, as one historian noted, "their voices were
lost in the void and Negroes were brought freely into all parts of
Indo-America."[34]

Thus the situation during the sixteenth and seventeenth
centuries was that although the Christian natural law teaching
was given considerable expression, it was not able to succeed in
checking an enslavement of the Negro. Rather, it was the
philosophy of the Enlightenment that finally won the battle for
the recognition of Negroes as human beings. It was the new,
eighteenth-century ideas regarding the equality and freedom of
all men—based on the observation and rationalism of the times—
that secured the emancipation, however temporary, of the
colored peoples. It should be cause for reflection to a church
whose only purpose is to preach the gospel of love, a church rich

in names like Thomas Aquinas, Bartholomew de Las Casas and a host of others, that it is the humanist writers such as Joseph Campillo de Cossio (1780) and Antonio de Ulloa (1748) who are most associated, at least on the continent of Europe, with the movement for the liberation of the colored peoples from slavery.

We have already shown that barriers to free migration are all too often simply those of race. Such barriers are entirely un-Christian. There are indeed circumstances—economic, cultural, and so forth—in which a limitation of migration may be necessary and legitimate. But it is never legitimate on the basis of race alone. For this is a form of racial discrimination which, if it is uncoupled (as it is *ex hypothesi*) with economic or cultural or other considerations, is the kind of "discrimination against" that is clearly unjust.

No race has been given exclusive hegemony over the earth or any part thereof. The Christian tradition concerning ownership of the goods of the earth applies, too, to occupation of the earth itself. Thus St. Ambrose preached, in his homily on Naboth's Vineyard, "Giving alms to the poor is not giving them what is yours, but rather a restitution of what is their own. . . . The earth belongs to all men, not to the rich alone."[35] Again, in his *De Officiis Ministrorum*, he says: "God ordered the earth to be the common possession of all. Nature therefore granted a common right. . . ."[36] And St. John Chrysostom put the same thing as follows: "It is common and not private property that has been given to us and is according to nature."[37]

Of course, these fathers of the early church had no intention of denying all right to private property. But what they did wish to insist on was that the original disposition of nature did not constitute a decision as to who was to own what. Private property, they knew, has many advantages, yet there are times when it should yield to the rights of the community or of individuals who find themselves in a situation of extreme need. St. Thomas

Aquinas defended the same idea: "Private property is not what is primarily laid down by nature, according to which all things are common."[38] At the same time, Aquinas maintained that the right to private property is a natural right.

This is what is meant by the descriptive assertion that private property is a "secondary natural right." In brief, there are occasions when it may be sacrificed in favor of common property, some occasions in fact when it should be so.

It is the same in the case of the occupancy of territory, whether by individuals or by nations or races. When faced with real need on the part of others, which can be met without undue disturbance, such occupancy has no right to be exclusive. Hence it is that immigration barriers that have no *raison d'être* other than a desire to discriminate against the occupancy of a given territory by members of another race are un-Christian on at least two important scores. For at one and the same time they offend against Christian principles about human equality and about the right of all men to live and move on the face of the earth. Christ himself, who enjoined us to love our neighbors as ourselves, has taught us, too, that our neighbor is every man.

Indeed we are rediscovering today, through the help of modern biblical scholarship, that what we have struggled for so long to express in complex philosophical language is stated in the Scriptures with stark simplicity: that in Christ God has called all men "son," and thus has established us all as brothers, one to another: "For to which of the angels has he ever said, 'Thou art my son, I this day have begotten thee'? and again, 'I will be to him a father, and he shall be to me a son'?" (Heb 1:5).

Notes

1. Trevor Huddleston, *Naught for Your Comfort* (London, 1956), p. 170.
2. Cited in *ibid.*, p. 169.
3. "Our Churches Sin Against the Negro," *Look*, May 18, 1965.

Cf. also Mgr. J. G. Chatham, "Religion and Race in the South," *The Catholic Mind*, LXIII (1965), No. 1193.

4. Cf. H. D. F. Kitto, *The Greeks* (New York, 1954; London, 1951), Ch. 1.

5. *Ibid.*, p. 9.

6. Cf. R. H. Barron, *The Romans* (London, 1949), pp. 170–171.

7. Cf. Kitto, *op. cit.*, p. 8.

8. *The Study of History* (Oxford, 1934), p. 247.

9. *Ibid.*, p. 224.

10. *Ibid.*, p. 211 seq.

11. Beatrix Lady Dunally, in *The Irish Independent*, November 20, 1963.

12. Cf. Karl Rahner, *Theological Investigations*, I (Baltimore, 1961). Cf. also Rahner, *Hominisation* (London, 1965), and Robert T. Francoeur, *Perspectives in Evolution* (Baltimore, 1965).

13. Cf. Y. M.-J. Congar, *The Catholic Church and the Race Question* (Paris, 1953), pp. 38–41.

14. *Ibid.*, pp. 40–41.

15. Cf. S. Zavala, *The Defense of Human Rights in Latin America* (Paris, 1964), pp. 15–24.

16. Cf. Lord Acton, *Lectures on Modern History* (New York, 1961).

17. Cf. Robert Wilberforce, *The Church and Slavery* (London, 1962), p. 7.

18. *Ibid.*, pp. 10–11.

19. *Ibid.*, pp. 16–17.

20. Cited in *ibid.*, p. 20.

21. Cf. L. Hanke, *Aristotle and the American Indians* (London, 1959).

22. Cf. Zavala, *op. cit.*, pp. 25–33.

23. Cited in *ibid.*, p. 31.

24. Cf. Hanke, *op. cit.*, p. 58.

25. Cited in Zavala, *op. cit.*, p. 42.

26. Cited in *ibid.*, p. 40.

27. Cited in *ibid.*, p. 41.

28. Cf. Hanke, *op. cit.*

29. Cf. L. Hanke, *Colonisation et conscience Chrétien au XVI siècle* (Paris, 1957), *passim*.

30. "The Supreme Court and Segregation," in *The Catholic Mind*, LV (1957).

31. Cf. Congar, *op. cit.*
Among the most powerful socio-moral condemnations of anti-

Semitism in modern times are the pastoral letter of the bishop of Linz (January, 1933), the pastoral letter of the Austrian hierarchy (December, 1933), the address of Cardinal Piazza, patriarch of Venice (January, 1939), and a number of statements by the French hierarchy during World War II. The objections of these documents stem first of all from the general grounds that anti-Semitism fails to give due respect to the human person and his natural rights, and secondly from the specific consideration that it involves unjust racial discrimination and/or persecution.

The Jewish problem, of course, is a spiritual as well as a sociological or political problem. "It would be a mistake," says Father Congar, "to regard the Hebrew community only as Jews, not as Israel . . . If the mystery of Israel were reduced to the sociological or political problem . . . Christians would run the risk of reducing Catholicism to a sociological phenomenon, a social religion."

Interesting points in connection with this have been made by the convert from Judaism, Friedmann, in his book *The Redemption of Israel*, and by Jean Daniélou in his book *Dialogue with Israel* (English translation published by Helicon, Baltimore and Dublin, 1967).

32. Listed in P. McKevitt, *The Plan of Society* (Dublin, 1944), p. 105.

33. Cited in Zavala, *op. cit.*, pp. 48–49.

34. Altamira, cited in *ibid.*, p. 50.

35. *Hom. de Nabuthe Jezraelita*, 1, 2. P.L. 14, 731.

36. *De Officiis*, 1, 28, 132. P.L. 16, 62.

37. *Epist. 1 ad Tim.*, Hom. 12, 4. P.G., 62, 564.

38. *In 4 Sent.*, D. 33, 2, 2, ql. 4, sol. 1. Cf. also *IIa IIae*, Q. 66, art. 2, obj. 1.

For Further Reading

O. de Férenzy, *Les Juifs et nous, chrétiens*, Paris, 1935.

Drostan Maclaren, O.P., *Private Property and the Natural Law*, Oxford, 1948.

C. M. Schroder, *Rasse und Religion*, Munich, 1937.

Mgr. Ed. Swanstrom "The Christian Attitude Toward Migration," in *Proceedings of the International Catholic Migration Congress*, Breda, 1954.

Race and Religion (A Symposium), London, 1966.

The Church and Contemporary Racism

However often the church as community has failed to react in a truly Christian manner to the problem of race, the voice of the church as institution has repeatedly condemned racism in all its forms. This is particularly true of the modern church and especially in the context of the color problem.

The Principles of Racial Justice

Time and again authoritative churchmen have spoken out against racial injustice. One of the first of our contemporaries was Archbishop Rummel of New Orleans in a pastoral letter read in all churches of his archdiocese on February 19, 1956. Already in 1955, the archbishop had given practical evidence of his attitude towards segregation. In what has come to be known as the "Jesuit Bend incident", parishioners in Jesuit Bend, Louisiana, refused to accept a Negro priest who had been sent as a replacement; Archbishop Rummel ordered the church closed until they modified their sentiments.

Then, in 1956, he gave his position theoretical utterance. In a strongly worded letter he entirely rejected racial segregation as something in conflict with the unity of the human race, the universality of the redemption, and the demands of justice and Christian love.[1] Racial segregation is in conflict with the unity and solidarity of the human race, said the archbishop, because of the emphasis of both the Old and the New Testaments that all mankind has a common father and mother in Adam and Eve, and one common destiny, namely to serve God and find eternal happiness with him in the world to come. Racial segregation is wrong, in the second place, because it is clearly a denial of the unity and universality of the redemption of Christ, who came into the world to save all men by making all members of his mystical body. Thirdly, racial segregation is morally wrong and sinful because it is both a violation of the rights of men as human beings and of the mandate of love of Christ to Christians.

What the archbishop here condemned is really unjust racial discrimination. He wrote: "To deny to members of a certain race, just because they are members of that race, certain rights and opportunities, civic or economic, educational or religious, recreational or social, imposes upon them definite hardships and humiliations, frustrations and impediments to progress which condemn them to perpetual degradation which is only a step removed from slavery."

Over the past ten years church statements by the hierarchies of the United States and South Africa make it abundantly clear that racial segregation as practiced in these countries is coincidental with unjust discrimination.

On July 20, 1957, the South African hierarchy issued an important condemnation of *apartheid*.[2] It is wrong, said the bishops, because its basic principle is the preservation of a white civilization that is identified with white supremacy, meaning the enjoyment of full social and political rights only by white men. While it is sometimes described as separate development, thus suggesting a system whereby different races are given the opportunity of pursuing their respective social and cultural evolutions, in reality the system as applied favors the white man. "It is agreed," said the bishops, "that only in this manner will these races be doing the will of God, lending themselves to the fulfillment of his providential designs. This contention sounds plausible as long as we overlook an important qualification, namely, that separate development is subordinate to white supremacy. The white man makes himself the agent of God's will and the interpreter of his providence in assigning the range and determining the bounds of non-white development."

One of the most far-reaching and best-known condemnations of racial segregation is that by the American hierarchy in 1958.[3] Recalling a previous statement, made in 1943, which called for justice and fair play for the Negro, and noting that considerable progress had been made in this direction in the years since then, the bishops went on to point out that, in recent times, progress towards the achievement of these goals had been slowed up, if not halted, in certain areas. Such developments, they said, are entirely un-Christian.

Directly raising the question as to whether enforced segregation can be reconciled with Christian principles, the bishops insisted that it cannot. They gave two fundamental reasons for this assertion. In the first place, by its very nature, all such compulsory segregation imposes a stigma of inferiority on the segregated people. For it implies a judgment to the effect that an entire race, by the sole fact of race and regardless of individual qualities, is unfit to associate on equal terms with members of another race. In the second place, whatever the theory, the hard fact is that segregation as practiced in the United States had led to the denial of basic human rights to the Negro, especially in the fields of education, job opportunity and housing. The famous doctrine of "separate but equal" treatment had not at all worked so as to avoid such evils. The statement continued:

> One of the tragedies of racial oppression is that the evils we have cited are being used as excuses to continue the very conditions that so strongly fostered such evils. Today we are told that Negroes, Indians, and also some Spanish-speaking Americans differ too much in culture and achievements to be assimilated in our schools, factories and neighborhoods. Some decades back the same charge was made against the immigrant Irish, Jewish, Italian, Polish, Hungarian, German, Russian. In every instance differences were used by some as a basis for discrimination and even for bigoted ill-treatment. The immigrant, fortunately, has

achieved his rightful status in the American community. Economic opportunity was wide open and educational equality was not denied to him. Negro citizens seek these same opportunities.

The American hierarchy's statement is concerned with "legal" or "compulsory" segregation, that is, segregation which involves "oppressive conditions" and "ill-treatment" for the racial group or groups at the receiving end of the legal process. Such segregation is indistinguishable from unjust discrimination. And that racial segregation as found in the United States and South Africa is indeed a form of unjust discrimination is the accusation of the Catholic hierarchies of these countries. Of course one sometimes finds attempts to justify such segregation. The following is an effort in this direction by the late Dr. Verwoerd: "The *apartheid* policy is one of getting the natives to grow from their own roots out of their own institutions and from their own powers. It is a policy of gradual development through mother tongue and own environment, to bring back the natives to literacy and usefulness in their own circle."[4]

In other words, so this argument runs, *compulsory* segregation is not always and *per se* unjust. Nobody has supplied a better answer to this than the American Jesuit Joseph Kenealy, who has been an intrepid fighter for the cause of racial justice. He writes:

1. The *per se* argument is an abstraction contemplating itself in a vacuum. It prescinds from the facts of life. It ignores the real problem in its moral and social context. The facts of life are that compulsory segregation is the product of the mentality of "racial supremacy." . . . Separate facilities are "inherently unequal," because the matrix and context of separation is the belief in the inequality of the separated. 2. The second answer to the *per se* argument is that, even supposing the contrary-to-fact hypothesis of equal facilities, compulsory segregation would still be objectively wrong; because it would still be contrary to the natural unity which impels human beings to associate in organized society for

the common good; because it would still violate the political and social unity of organized society which is demanded, in both justice and charity, by the essential equality and natural dignity of human personality.[5]

One is reminded of Pope Pius XII's words, in the encyclical *Summi Pontificatus* of October 20, 1939, to the effect that the human race, though divided in virtue of the natural order established by God into social groups, nations and states independent one of another as far as concerns the organization and regulation of their internal life, is nonetheless united by mutual bonds, moral and judicial, in one great community. It was in virtue of these same considerations that Bishop Robert E. Lucey of San Antonio spoke of the "sin of racial segregation" and ordered the integration of the schools of his archdiocese in 1954[6]; that, in March, 1952, Monsignor Henri Varin de la Brunelière, bishop of Martinique, castigated the anti-racialism involved in colonialism; and that the bishops of Tanganyika did the same thing in July, 1953.[7]

The Need for Gradualism in Racial Integration

The fact that it is a Christian duty to reject all forms of racial discrimination—including segregation—does not at all mean that one should be impetuous about effecting integration. The hidden difficulties that lie in the path of this are laid bare only to a calm appraisal of what exactly one means when one speaks of integration.

Philip Mason, director of the British Institute of Race Relations, in a penetrating analysis of what is meant by integration, has discussed it in terms of absorption, assimilation and accommodation, adaptation and acceptance.[8] Absorption means complete disappearance, as happened for example, to eighteenth-century Negroes in London. Assimilation, on the other hand, is less far-reaching. An assimilated group will disperse and mingle with the rest of the population, dropping their cultural distinc-

tiveness and keeping only their surnames and physical characteristics. This is what has happened the vast majority of European
immigrants into the United States.

It goes without saying, of course, that integration presupposes,
if not assimilation or absorption, at least some effort at adaptation
on the part of the group to be integrated and at accommodation
on the part of the group integrated into. Some groups shun
assimilation, as is the case, for example, with Jews and Gypsies.
But they do not refuse all adaptation. Indeed the Jews are
usually expert at this within the framework of their own selective
scale. Accommodation is the correlative of adaptation and while
it represents the effort made by each group to adapt itself to the
other, it is perhaps most frequently used by the receiving group.
It inevitably entails some degree of acceptance. Thus the
indigenous group may accept immigrants as workmates but
refuse to have anything to do with them socially. Only when
accommodation has been effected in every respect is it possible
to say that there has been full acceptance. So also full adaptation
and assimilation.

It is quite obvious, therefore, that integration, in so far as it
entails adaptation and accommodation, must take time before it
can be full and complete. And it is clear too that, while it
absolutely demands a considerable degree of adaptation and
accommodation, it is not at all the same as either assimilation or
complete absorption. Integration is compatible with a good deal
of cultural and other pluralism, as is evident in the case of the
French Canadians or that of the Parsees of Bombay. The latter
case especially provides an excellent example of distinctive dress,
special rites, successful though unpopular trading activities—yet
all without causing any general hostility and in a way that must
be classed as truly integrated. In this sense integration is as
eminently compatible with a multi-racial as with a non-racial
society.

Indeed it is Philip Mason's argument that modern society is

to an ever greater extent a collection of groupings of all kinds. Groupings also that are not at all self-contained. Nor exclusive, for that matter, either. Some are based on politics, some on economics, some on religion, leisure, and so on. As a member of his political group a man may be quite cut off from the members of other political groups, but he may be intimately associated with some of them in a leisure group. This has importance not only for better mixing but also for the judgments which people pass on each other. For it means simply that there is more than one scale of reference on which to judge, and success in one can redeem low rating in another.

Mason translates all this on to the present-day British scene by protesting that he is all for diverse groups and subgroups— societies for Welsh madrigals, Pakistani festivals, West Indian cricket clubs, Calypsos and steel bands—but on the one condition that no one be denied entry to one group on the sole ground that he belongs to another. He concludes:

> What we should hope, then, I suggest, is that the immigrant groups now in Britain—Sikhs, Gujeratis, Pakistanis from the Punjab, Pakistanis from Bengal, Jamaicans, Trinidadians, small islanders—will form a variety of groups, some wider, some smaller, and that they will retain some of their cultural traits. But we hope that members of these groups will also join other groups, trade unions, cricket and hockey clubs, churches, concert parties. The object should be a steady increase in the two processes of adaptation and acceptance until a stage is reached in mutual accommodation which may be called inclusion. This would be integration but not assimilation.

It stands to reason, therefore, that there is need for great prudence in working towards racial integration. To move too fast could mean an upsetting of the processes of adaptation and accommodation which are so essential for the development of a desirable form of integration. For these processes have their own rate of dynamism, related to the real and often deep-seated

differences which exist between people, especially people of
different race.

In their 1957 statement, the bishops of South Africa were very
careful to draw attention to this. As they put it themselves, the
condemnation of the principle of *apartheid* cannot mean that
perfect equality can be established in South Africa "by a stroke
of the pen." The profound differences between sections of the
population make immediate total integration impossible. People
must have much more in common culturally before they can
share equally in the same political and economic institutions.

Hence, "all social change must be gradual if it is not to be
disastrous." For this reason the bishops declared that it would be
unreasonable to condemn all South Africa's differential legislation. They were conscious, however, of the fact that many of
those who suffered under the system of *apartheid* would find it
hard to accept counsels of moderation. Embittered by years of
frustration, such people distrust any policy which involves a
gradual change. They see redress only in the sweeping away of
all differences, by revolution not evolution. But the bishops
warned of the dangers in their attitude: "A gradual change it
must be: gradual, for no other kind of change is compatible with
the maintenance of order, without which there is no society, no
government, no justice, no common good. But a change must
come, for otherwise our country faces a disastrous future."

In their 1958 statement, the American bishops spoke in like
fashion, urging that concrete plans for racial integration be based
on prudence, the "virtue that inclines us to view problems in
their proper perspective." In the American context, they went
on to say immediately, this means a realization that today's
problems in the racial field are rooted in decades, even centuries
of custom. Changes in such deep-rooted cultural patterns "are
not made overnight."

For this reason, continued the American bishops, it is not a sign of weakness to watch one's step, to recognize some changes as being more necessary than others or, what is even more important, some more capable of achievement than others. It is true that "a gradualism that is merely a cloak for inaction" is to be deplored. But one must equally deplore a rash impetuosity that would sacrifice solid achievements for ill-considered or premature ventures. Prudence and rashness must be distinguished between by seeking the considered judgment of experienced counsellors.

Hence the American hierarchy appealed to its people—indeed to all responsible and sober-minded Americans of all religious faiths—to take the role of leadership into their own reliable hands and thus thwart the agitators and the racists. They concluded: "All must act quietly, and prayerfully before it is too late."

In other words, there is need on the part of both state and church for the conception and implementation of a rational plan for the ending of racial segregation.

"Intransigent" and "Progressive" Attitudes to Integration

The problem is more easily posed than resolved. On the one hand there are those intransigents for whom even a gradual ending of segregation is a sell-out that is too much to be asked to bear. Such, for example, were the members of a Catholic group in New Orleans who sent an appeal to Pope Pius XII in 1957 requesting a halt to church activities in racial integration. This group, calling itself the Association of Catholic Laymen of New Orleans, appealed directly to the pope, asking that, pending a papal announcement, Archbishop Rummel be requested to take no further steps towards integration. They also asked that the pontiff issue a decree stating that segregation is not "morally wrong and sinful" as it had been described by the archbishop. Such tactics, of course, only drew from sources "close to the Vatican" a reiteration of the fact that the church had on many occasions shown itself to be unswervingly opposed to racial discrimination. But the incident illustrates the extreme elements that are liable to appear, in the church as elsewhere, as soon as even careful and measured steps are taken towards racial integration. And how deep this extremism can run is evidenced by the fact that some New Orleans Catholics accepted excommunication rather than the archbishop's ruling.

On the other hand, there are those, white and Negro, who are impatient for integration, following the leadership of Dr. Martin Luther King. For these a policy of gradualism is not fast enough, although they do not subscribe to a policy of physical force. The position of this group was well put by Dr. King himself when he said: "People have to understand that the choice is no longer between nice little meetings and non-violence. It is between militant non-violence and riots."[9] And the very title of Dr. King's book, *Why We Can't Wait*, is indicative of this basic thesis. In the chapter "A Letter from Birmingham Jail," he expresses his reaction to the appeal to "wait": "We have waited more than 340 years for our constitutional and God-given rights." It is clear that much can be said in favor of a rapid policy of integration.[10]

The South African hierarchy has taken concrete steps in an effort to combat *apartheid* in their country.[11] In their 1957 statement they indicated that they had no intention of allowing *apartheid* to continue as a feature of church practice itself. "The practice of segregation," they said, "though not officially recognized in our churches, characterizes, nevertheless, many of our church societies, our schools, seminaries, convents, hospitals and the social life of our people. In the light of Christ's teaching this cannot be tolerated forever. The time has come to pursue more vigorously the change of heart and practice that the law of Christ demands. We are hypocrites if we condemn *apartheid* in South African society and condone it in our own institutions."[12]

Shortly after this, they issued a declaration that "Catholic churches must and shall remain open to all without regard to their racial origin." This directive ran head-on against a new national law to the contrary, the so-called "Church Clause" of the Native Laws Amendment Act.

By their 1957 statements the hierarchy made it quite plain that they regarded government policy in this matter as intrinsically evil, while they also set about eliminating as much *apartheid* as possible within the confines of the church itself. The precise position of *apartheid* in church-run institutions was then open, and is still open, to some question. At the time we are speaking of, 1957, Andrew J. Murray, managing editor of *The Southern Cross*, the Capetown Catholic weekly, told the N.C.W.C. News Service that he had yet to come across an example of *apartheid* in a South African Catholic Church. Generally, he said, all races worshiped side by side. But in some mission churches, where congregations were overwhelmingly composed of African natives, it was the whites who might worship separately, say in a side chapel. The primitive Bantu faithful, however devout and fervent, lived very close to nature and had different habits of hygiene from those of European extraction—an explanation at least, if not an excuse, for this separation. But where whites predominated, *apartheid* in churches was rare.

Further testimony came from reporters of the native weekly *Drum*, who visited various "white" churches to see what would happen. They were ejected from some Dutch Reformed Churches but had no complaints about Catholic ones. Catholic schools, on the other hand, have been, without exception, conducted on racial lines. This has been defended in general on the debatable grounds that, by and large, the African native and the white South African represent very different levels of culture and civilization. As we have seen, the system all too easily only serves to perpetuate this situation. In many cases, however, the reason for the separation is that—unlike the mission schools—many white Catholic schools depend on state grants, which would unquestionably be withdrawn if the church tried to introduce integration. But whatever the Catholic ideal or the wishes of the bishops, the real reason for the continued existence of segregation in church schools is that if non-white pupils were introduced into a white school, that school would soon have no white pupils left. In 1957 a Catholic weekly newspaper could report that "in general, very few South Africans—even those with great goodwill towards the African—are psychologically ready for integration. And thus far the church here has accepted the fact that if she is to have white children in her schools they must be separate. The same applies to many Catholic lay societies."[13]

This situation drew much criticism on the heads of the bishops after their collective statements on the problem in 1957. As a result, Durban's Archbishop Hurley expressed the hope that clergy and laity would face the matter together "with true prudence, true courage and the true mind of Christ." While stressing that there must be a clear intention of working towards the application of Catholic principles, he added that "the Church understands human nature and knows that a hasty application may sometimes do more harm than good." In Capetown, Archbishop McCann said: "We do not ask for a revolutionary change, but we ask for a change of heart and approach. . . . Some may say that we must root out what is evil immediately, but that, too, would be unjust as well as unreasonable. Almighty God is more aware than we are of the evil in the world, but he does not destroy those who work it. He instead brings good out of evil. The church has to work patiently to overcome evil by good."[14]

It seems, however, that since 1957 Archbishop Hurley has come to realize that the ending of segregation has been going far too slowly in South Africa. In his 1964 Hoernle Memorial Lecture, given under the auspices of the South African Institute of Race Relations in Johannesburg, he called for a crusade against *apartheid:*

Let us make no mistake about it—only crusaders succeed in the field of social reform. It takes drive and dynamism to alter a social pattern. If Christianity wants to have any say in the alteration of South Africa's social pattern, its representatives will have to become crusaders, crusaders fully possessed of that which is characteristic of crusaders—a flame of conviction, fire or zeal. It will take all that to enable any Christian who takes the Christian ethics seriously in South Africa to make an impact on white Christian societies surrounding him, for that white Christian society has grown up in the firm conviction that the law of love does not apply to non-Europeans, except in special and unusual circumstances.[15]

Inter-Episcopal Differences about Apartheid in South Africa?

According to the London *Observer*, it was with a view to disassociating himself from these views of Archbishop Hurley that Archbishop Whelan of Bloemfontein, during the month following Archbishop Hurley's lecture, made a statement on *apartheid* that seemed to run counter to his fellow bishop's in important respects.[16] Among Archbishop Whelan's points were that the theory of *apartheid* is not in itself vicious, that the teaching of the church need not necessarily be opposed to it, that it cannot be said that the curtailment of the individual's rights constitutes necessarily an injustice in all circumstances, and that the Catholic Church is concerned to defend the rights of minorities throughout the world. Speaking to the South African Press Association the archbishop declared that the church was not opposed to "the idea of a state composed of a number of national or racial groups maintained in their separate and distinct identity." On the contrary, he said, "The church regards as immoral any policy aimed at levelling ethnic groups into an amorphous cosmopolitan mass."

This statement caused a flurry of comment in the world's press. In general the matter was written up as evidence of a Catholic split on the question of *apartheid* in South Africa. *The Observer*, for example, spoke of the "archbishop's evident concern to justify the South African government's policy . . . [and] to minimize differences between the Roman Catholics and the Dutch Reformed Church." As far as public opinion goes at least, the matter was cleared up a week later when the South African hierarchy, meeting in conference in Pretoria, affirmed its opposition to *apartheid*, confirmed that the official policy of the South African bishops in respect to race relations was that set out in earlier statements in 1952, 1957 and after, and declared that statements on race relations made by individual bishops "are made on their own responsibilities."[17]

From a doctrinal point of view, however, Archbishop Whelan's statement is found upon close reading to be less contradictory than it seems. Theoretically there is nothing about segregation in itself that makes it necessarily and unavoidably immoral; strictly speaking it is the social separation of two groups and should bear equally on—and indeed could even be welcomed by—both. It is only in so far as it is imposed by one group on the other in an objectionable way that it comes to constitute unjust discrimination.

Archbishop Hurley, on the other hand, while he did not deny this, was acutely aware that the argument was rather doctrinaire. What he was concerned with was that, as found in South Africa, segregation is indeed unjust discrimination. That his lecture was essentially an exercise in applied rather than speculative ethics is something as undeniable as it is important for an understanding of it. Take, for example, the following passage:

> There are many politicians, I am sure, who are prepared . . . to meet religious critics on their own grounds and to argue the case with honesty and sincerity that *apartheid* properly understood is acceptable to the Christian conscience. This kind of *apartheid* is separate development. . . . It remains to consider, therefore, whether or not injustice is inherently involved in the policy of separate development as it is being currently pursued. . . . To justify the moral acceptability of separate development it would appear that there are four conditions which must be demonstrated

as possible of fulfillment: first, the policy must be feasible; second, it must meet with the free consent of all parties involved; third, there must be a proportionate share of sacrifice; and fourth, the rights of all parties must be adequately protected during the transition period.

Needless to say, Archbishop Hurley had no difficulty in showing that *apartheid* as it is practiced in South Africa does not at all satisfy these four conditions. And although Archbishop Whelan did not go into the matter in such detail in his statement, nothing that he said was inconsistent with Archbishop Hurley's tests.[18] Both prelates pointed out that the present sacrifices are disproportionate and that the Bantu are suffering hardship rather than being protected during the transitional period. Where they differed seemed to be in the application of the first two conditions to the facts. Whereas Archbishop Whelan seemed to imply that it is a practical possibility to create separate African states, or Bantustans, on the lines of the present experiment of the Transkei area, Archbishop Hurley was doubtful about the kind of independence, economic or otherwise, that would be conferred on such states by South Africa.

Certainly, as far as the present Bantustan is concerned, no real independence has been conferred. Nor indeed does it seem— as Archbishop Hurley pointed out—that anybody in South Africa is in favor of it, whether Africans or Europeans. Yet the London *Tablet's* commentary on the matter is both interesting and important:

The most charitable commentary . . . is that it is unfair to reach any final conclusion on either feasibility or consent unti the Transkei experiment has lasted for two or three years. . . . If the South African government were to end its policy of curtailing both industrial and educational opportunities in Transkei; if it were to compensate every family settled there even to the same extent as the assisted passage money which it gives to European immigrants, it is not impossible that more Africans would give their consent to the idea of separate development. If the government agreed to a federal relationship between Transkei and Basutoland, which, combined, might opt for a special link with the British Crown, the policy would come nearer to feasibility. For without the active economic and technological support of the outside world none of the Bantustans can ever become genuinely independent.[19]

The Race Question at Vatican II

The most recent authoritative Roman teaching on the race question prior to Vatican Council II was that contained in the encyclical *Pacem in Terris*. "It is a demand of truth," said Pope John, "that discrimination because of racial origin does not come into the picture to distort it: that we therefore cling firmly to the principle that all states are equal as regards their natural dignity." *Pacem in Terris* rejects both racial discrimination and racist theories, in both their individual and their political manifestations.[20] While admitting realistically that there are undoubted differences between individual men, Pope John insisted that these inequalities are no excuse for the more fortunate to lord it over their neighbors by way of discriminating against them simply on the basis of these differences. In the matter of superiority and inferiority, he is adamant that there are no grounds whatever for racial discrimination. All individual human beings are equal as men; all political communities are equal as political communities. There are none that are superior or inferior simply by their nature. Truth in relations between states, therefore, strictly enjoins that racial discrimination and race theories be eliminated. In his encyclical, Pope John adverted to the fact that peoples can be, and are rightly, sensitive to their rights and dignity in this respect in such a way that there can be little doubt that he had in mind relations with racial minorities within a single state as well as those between nation states as a whole.

The race issue came up again at the ecumenical council. During the third session, and particularly in the course of the debate on the schema on the church in the modern world, many prelates from the United States, India and Africa asked the council to speak out strongly against racial discrimination in all its forms. Archbishop Patrick O'Boyle of Washington, D.C., speaking for the 175 United States bishops in Rome, called on the church to do everything in its power "to eliminate the cancerous evil of racial injustice." He asked that a special section on this problem be added to the fourth chapter of the council's draft decree, "The Church in the Modern World." Bishop Andrew Grutka of Indiana gave examples of the evils of racial segregation in the United States. He said that the church's image had been tarnished because of it. "The pastoral labors of the priests have been vitiated, and the apostolic work of missionaries stymied, because of parishioners abandoning their neighborhoods when people of another color attempt to settle there," he declared. Likewise an Indian archbishop spoke out against *apartheid* and the color bar, while an African archbishop said that crimes such as racism came from a disregard for human dignity.[21]

This was during the debate of October 28th. On October 24th the council had already heard Bishop Robert E. Treacy of Baton Rouge, Louisiana, speaking in the name of all members of the United States hierarchy at the council meeting, demand a special council declaration against racial discrimination.[22] He noted that the text of the schema "The Church in the Modern World," while stating that there can be no inequality among members of the church because of national origins, social class or sex, had failed to make reference to race, and asked that the text be amended to include this. He declared:

> The inclusion of this point would emphasize that equality which is enjoyed by all the members of the people of God in the Christian economy. No discrimination based on racial considerations can be reconciled with the truth whereby we believe that God creates all men equal in rights and dignity. . . . If this

change is made it will be easier for bishops to provide their faithful with the proper instruction on the question of race prejudice.
It would also reassure those who have been humiliated or have
been deprived of natural rights because of racial prejudice. In
addition, it would serve as a basis for important future declarations of the council.

At the United States bishops' press panel, Bishop Treacy said
that he had actually been speaking in the name of the entire
American hierarchy. He said that he had been authorized to do
so at the hierarchy's meeting of October 21st. He explained that
147 United States bishops had affixed their signatures to the
petition which was attached to his speech when he presented it
to the council's secretariat.

It seems fair to say that their attitude in the matter of race at
the council was the reflection of a growing uneasiness on the part
of the bishops of the United States to the general slowness of
the nation in implementing the civil rights bill. In March, 1963,
for example, the archbishop of Baltimore, Laurence J. (now
Cardinal) Shehan, had issued a pastoral letter complaining that
"our proposed state law of equal accommodations has thus far
been emasculated by our state legislators" and expressing his
concern that there should be no racial segregation in churches,
schools, hospitals or diocesan organizations and institutions of
all kinds. Other bishops put out similar pastorals.

Later, in August of the same year, a climax to this series of
individual pronouncements came in the form of a historic joint
pastoral letter from the hierarchy as a whole.[23] Its primary
purpose was to offer "some pastoral suggestions for a Catholic
approach to racial harmony." Condemning all forms of discrimination and segregation based on prejudice, the bishops
counselled Catholics:

> It is our strict duty to respect the basic human rights of every
> person. We know that public authority is obliged to help correct
> the evils of unjust discrimination practiced against any group or

class. We also recognize that every minority group in America seeking its lawful rights has the obligation of respecting the lawful rights of others. No Catholic with a good Christian conscience can fail to recognize the rights of all citizens to vote. Moreover, we must provide for all equal opportunity for employment, full participation in our public and private educational facilities, proper housing and adequate welfare assistance when needed.

Appealing for action to increase knowledge of the attitudes among both races before action is taken to correct inequities, the bishops continued:

We can show our Christian charity by a quiet and courageous determination to make the quest for racial harmony a matter of personal involvement. We must go beyond slogans and generalizations about color and realize that all of us are human beings, men, women and children, all sharing the same human nature and dignity, with the same desires, hopes and feelings. We should try to know and understand one another.

By way of detailing how free exchange of ideas between races can be carried out, the bishops said that people in the same line of work should discuss problems caused by racial barriers. "Physicians of one race can talk with those of another. So can businessmen, teachers, lawyers, secretaries, farmers, clerks and other workers." Catholic parish and diocesan societies, along with political gatherings and civic associations, could also provide the "common meeting grounds" that are needed.

We may act through various lay organizations of the church as well as with civic groups of every type. In many parts of the nation there are interracial committees representing the major religious faiths as well as important aspects of civic life. We bless and endorse such efforts.

Reverend Martin Luther King and Father Trevor Huddleston

This episcopal statement was issued just about the time that Martin Luther King was beginning to recommend direct action, including civil disobedience, to push integration. It was in April, 1963, in his famous "Letter from Birmingham Jail," that he had so severely criticized the attitude of the man who is inclined to temporize in the matter of racial justice, "who paternalistically believes he can set the time table for another man's freedom; who lives by a mythical concept of time and who constantly advises the Negro to wait for 'a more convenient season,' " the man who says that "the teachings of Christ take time to come to earth." "Such an attitude," said Dr. King, "stems from a tragic mis-conception of time," the false belief that it inevitably cures all ills.[24] For Dr. King the matter is clear and simple: Segregation destroys the "I-thou" relationship spoken of by the Jewish philosopher Martin Buber, and substitutes for it an "I-it" re-lationship which relegates persons to the status of things. The hard fact is that the segregation laws are morally unjust and, because of this, and here he recalls the words of St. Augustine, they cannot rightly be said to be laws at all. The true Christian, therefore, must refuse to obey them. Because of its failure to inculcate civil disobedience of this kind, Dr. King declared that he was "greatly disappointed with the white Church and its leadership."

Martin Luther King's approach, however militant, is essen-tially one of non-violence. A similar policy has been recom-mended by Father Trevor Huddleston in South Africa. It is Father Huddleston's view that it is not enough to speak about theology; to confine oneself to this, he says, would be to lose the struggle. There is need to use political weapons, to employ force, at least in the sense of a spiritual boycott of those who are opposed to racial integration. For Christians are free to use such force. To think otherwise is to have an entirely defective under-standing of the true meaning of Christian love. Surely it cannot be said that Christians must absolutely avoid everything that would wound the susceptibilities of others, that they must avoid all forms of criticism, avoid arousing even the consciences of

fellow Christians to what is wrong? Why is it, asks Father
Huddleston, that "to so many the figure of Christ is the figure
of the 'pale Galilean,' whose meekness and gentleness are utterly
incompatible with any conception of anger against social evil or
individual pride?"[25]

And so while Father Huddleston declares that he does not
know how long it will take before the evil of racial injustice is
eradicated, and while he does not believe it to be a part of the
Christian's responsibility to prophesy the circumstances of
historical change, he does insist that God is not mocked and that
every God-fearing man and genuine Christian must be committed
as a partisan in the struggle for racial justice. Father Huddleston
himself quite frankly admits that if his attitude means disloyalty
to South Africa, then he is prepared to be disloyal. He prefers
to believe that "Christians are called to a higher obedience."

The Church Has Its Chance—Now

And so the debate goes on, as to what is the best practical policy
for Christians to adopt when confronted with the problem of
race. While allowing for the need for prudence and an ordered
and harmonious approach to the matter, as recommended by the
joint pastoral letter of the American bishops, it should not be
forgotten either that there is no time to lose. This is something
on which all are agreed. In his 1965 Godfrey Day Memorial
Lectures in Dublin, Right Reverend Dr. Joost de Blank, Canon
of Westminster and formerly Anglican archbishop of Capetown,
stressed the need for the church to have a full involvement
in the world of today and criticized the Dutch Reformed Church
in South Africa for keeping silent in the matter of *apartheid*. "In
this day and age," he said, "there are times when, in the course
of events, it is the duty of the church to speak out in the name of
Christ, whether such counsel was popular or unpopular. There
exists a danger to the church of compromise—compromise with
money, politics and nationalism—and it is the church's duty to

guard against this compromise with all the sincerity and attention at its command."[26]

Speaking of the American situation, Robert W. Spike has said that during 1963 and 1964 the churches have gained themselves a reprieve in the matter of race by establishing inter-religious conferences on religion and race, strongly supporting the Civil Rights Bill, and rallying people behind demonstrations such as the one at Selma. For him the question is: "Can the momentum be maintained?" He replies, "Only if the churches find ways to help bring about changes in housing patterns, job opportunity, school balancing and up-grading, will they fulfill the promises made by their participation in the early stages of the Negro revolution."[27] In other words, the church must seek to avoid a failure analogous to that of the French revolution; while giving theoretical assent to the three-pronged program of "liberty, equality and fraternity," in practice it failed to secure anything other than an empty political liberty, thus allowing socialism to get the credit later for being the effective champion of equality and brotherhood. It is Spike's opinion that the real test for the church is yet to come, in the period immediately ahead.

One thing can be said with certainty: neither side has anything to gain by physical force. It was Carl Rowan, head of the United States Information Agency, who once said that "bayonets are very educational." But although from time to time—as during the Los Angeles riots—it has been found necessary to call for the use of them by National Guardsmen to restore order, white Americans in general do not look to this means to solve the problem. Similarly, even though Mississippi has produced terrorist organizations, like the Russian Nihilists and the Stern Gang of Palestine, and even though according to Brink and Harris's *The Negro Revolution in America*, 52 percent of all Negro Americans think that if things came to gunfighting, the Negro would win, the vast majority of their leaders do not.[28] On the other hand, through the use of moral power, he can win, for then, by the white man's own professed standards, he is indisputably in the right.

Notes

1. Cf. Most Rev. Joseph Francis Rummel, "The Morality of Racial Segregation," in *The Catholic Mind*, May, 1956.
2. The South African Hierarchy, "Race Relations," in *The Catholic Mind*, March-April, 1958.
3. Cf. "On Racial Discrimination," N.C.W.C., 1958.
4. Cited in Trevor Huddleston, *Naught for Your Comfort* (London, 1956), p. 42.
5. Cf. *The Catholic Mind*, LV (1957).
6. Cf. *The Catholic Mind*, LII (1954).
7. Cf. R. Delavignette, *Christianity and Colonialism* (London, 1964).
8. Philip Mason, "What Do We Mean by Integration?," in *New Society*, June 16, 1966.
9. As reported in *The New York Times* (International Edition), July 11, 1966.
10. Cf. also Hans Habe, *The Wounded Land* (New York, 1964); British edition, *The Anatomy of Hatred* (London, 1964).
11. Cf. reports in *Zeelandia*, August 8, 1957 and September 12, 1957.
12. *Loc. cit.*
13. *Zeelandia*, August 8, 1957.
14. Cf. *Zeelandia*, September 12, 1957.
15. Archbishop Denis E. Hurley, "Apartheid: Crisis of Christian Conscience," in *The Catholic Mind*, LXII, No. 1182.
16. Cf. *The Observer* (London), February 23, 1964.
17. Cf. *The Irish Independent*, February 28, 1964.
18. Cf. "The Church and Apartheid," in *The Tablet* (London), February 29, 1964.
19. *Loc. cit.* On July 26, 1966 the South African hierarchy again presented a united front in a pastoral published after a plenary session of the Bishops Conference. This document once more blasted *apartheid* as a most unjust form of racial discrimination. While appreciating what had been done in the fields of housing, education, health and social welfare to alleviate the situation of the Africans, it

was categorical that much more remained to be done. Cf. *The Tablet*, August 6, 1966.

Immediately 33 Anglican clergymen signed a letter supporting the bishops' joint pastoral. The letter, which appeared in the morning daily, *The Cape Times*, said that the signatories rejoiced greatly at the new condemnation of racial discrimination, particularly as "too little is being done both in Anglican and other South African Churches" to counteract this. Among the signatories was the Anglican suffragan bishop of Capetown, Philip Russell. Cf. *The Universe*, August 5, 1966.

20. Cf. J. Newman, *Principles of Peace* (Oxford, 1964), p. 134 seq.
21. As reported in *The Irish Independent*, October 29, 1964.
22. Cf. report in *Zeelandia*, October 31, 1963.
23. Cf. report in *The Advocate*, August 29, 1963.
24. Cf. *Why We Can't Wait* (New York, 1963), pp. 81–85.
25. *Op. cit.*, pp. 172–175.
26. As reported in *The Irish Times*, January 30, 1965.
27. In *Look*, May 18, 1965.
28. Cited in Robert Penn Warren, "The Negro Now," in *Look*, March 23, 1965.

For Further Reading

"Catholics and Race Bias," in *America*, CVIII (1963).

H. L. Cooper, "Priests, Prejudice and Race," in *The Catholic Mind*, Nov.-Dec., 1959.

A. Foley, S.J., "Racism and the Catholic Intellectual," in *Integrity*, June, 1956.

C. Hill, *West Indian Migrants and the London Churches*, Oxford, 1966.

G. P. Hughes, "Selected Bibliography of Writings on Racism by Catholic Authors," in *The Catholic Library World*, XXXIII (1961).

J. H. Kirk, "The Social Conscience of the Christian South," in *Social Compass*, XIII (1966), No. 4.

Archbishop Patrick O'Boyle, "The Racial Apostolate," in *The Interracial Review*, XXXIII (1960).

V. J. Reed, "You Are All One," in *The Catholic Mind*, January, 1962.

The Church and Migration

One of the subjects in which the Holy See has shown itself most interested since the second world war is the whole question of migration and its implications. It has sought to arouse the conscience of Catholics and of the nations of the world to a sense of responsibility in dealing with the problems which migration creates. In 1951, at the special request of Pope Pius XII, the International Catholic Migration Commission was formed. With headquarters at Geneva, it serves as an agency for the co-ordination, information and representation of the Catholic effort to meet migration problems. Its congresses have contributed much towards the drawing up of a Catholic migration policy.

The Holy See itself has issued a number of important statements on principles. It has rightly been said that the precepts which Pius XII offered to the world on the subject of migration had never before been presented so fully.[1] They cover both what the pope called "forced migration," that is, of exiles or refugees on the move for political reasons, and "natural migration," that is, migration that is due to lack of space or a lack of adequate means of subsistence.

In August, 1952, he issued *Exsul Familia*, an apostolic constitution on the spiritual care of emigrants. In many addresses, he dealt with the problems of emigration. He explained the church's interest in this issue in an address to an International Congress on Migration held at Naples in October, 1951:

We feel called upon to tell you that the Catholic Church feels itself obliged to take the greatest interest in the work of migration. This involves finding a remedy for pressing needs—the lack of space and the lack of the means of existence because a fatherland of former years is no longer able to nourish her children and over-population compels them to emigrate; the misery of those fleeing or driven from their homeland, of millions compelled to renounce their native land and to journey afar to search for and find for themselves another. The Church feels her distress all the more since, in very large measure, it is her own children that are in-volved.

In pursuit of this objective the Holy See and many Catholic organizations have started practical activities directed at aiding migrants and refugees. Regional offices of the International Catholic Migration Commission have been established in many Latin American countries. The American National Catholic Welfare Conference has also extended its work in regard to migration. Days specially dedicated to the emigrant, or immi-grant, as the circumstances may demand, are celebrated in Italy, Malta and the Netherlands, Argentina and Venezuela. In Canada, too, a special Immigration Day is celebrated on January 6th each year. In Australia, on Social Justice Sunday, the bishops annually remind their people of their duties as Catholics towards immi-grants. Everywhere public opinion is being educated about migration problems by lectures, congresses and the dissemina-tion of news by the International Catholic Migration Commission.

Although there is no specific set of Catholic principles which relate exclusively to racial migration, all of the church's migration principles and policies, in one way or another, are relevant to it.

Catholic Principles on Migration

From the papal addresses and Catholic migration agencies which we have mentioned, it is possible to derive a body of principles which represents what might be called the Catholic approach to migration problems. A complete policy has not yet been formulated, since the subject is still a developing one and the principles are fashioned as concrete problems arise. Nevertheless, it will be profitable to survey the whole Catholic approach to migration and the principles by which practical efforts should be guided.

First of all, what is the Catholic attitude to migration in general? It was well summed up by Monsignor Rodhain of the French *Secours Catholique* in a short paper to the International Catholic Migration Congress at Breda in 1954.[2] The first thing which must be remembered, said Monsignor Rodhain, is that the earth was given by God to all men to enable them to lead a life that will conduce to salvation. Therefore for any group to arbitrarily close the frontiers of its territories to others is unequivocally inhuman and unjust. Secondly, however, it must be remembered that the countries of the world consist of organized communities and nations. In the measure in which this is true, a migrant has no right to impose himself on a country without accepting its just laws and striving to integrate himself into the community which he finds there. These are considerations which flow clearly and immediately from the twin orders of charity and justice. In addition, there are the orders of providence and of redemption. One could regard the phenomenon of migration as merely the consequence of economic or political disorders. But, said Monsignor Rodhain, there is an important sense in which these factors themselves are subordinate to a higher purpose—"increase and multiply and fill the earth" (Gen 1:28). Thus he pointed out the significance that migration has from the point of view of redemption and the growth and vigor of the mystical body of Christ.

The standards by which migration may be adjudged successful from the Catholic point of view are threefold.[3] First of all, the preservation of religious integrity. It was with this that Pius XII was especially concerned in *Exsul Familia*. It involves the special preparation of the migrant before leaving his country of origin, so that the new pattern of life in the country to which he is going may not prove injurious, if not fatal, to his religious practice.

Secondly, the integrity of the family must be safeguarded. There are special dangers attendant on the migration system under which the breadwinner goes abroad and is separated from wife and family for indefinite periods. It must be the constant object of Catholic migration activities to seek to bring about the reunion of such families.

Thirdly, there is the preservation of cultural integrity. Migration studies have conclusively proved that one's sense of human dignity can be considerably diminished by the feeling of losing one's cultural traditions. Language, culture and traditions are a part of a man's personality and he should not be required to strip himself of them, at least immediately, when he migrates from his mother country to another. Ideally he should integrate himself into his new milieu eventually, but the process should be gradual and discriminating and of such a nature as will allow, in so far as is possible, the co-existence of varied cultural patterns.

At the concrete level the Catholic attitude may be expressed as follows. As regards emigration: a) no country has the right to place obstacles to those of its citizens who, for good reasons, may wish to leave it and live elsewhere; b) if emigration is a necessity for large numbers of its citizens, a country should help them to emigrate and to settle down in their new home. As regards immigration: a) underdeveloped countries should open their doors to all serious applications on the part of immigrants; b) they should also help them to settle down after their arrival.

It is the church's policy to try to bring about more human legal arrangements in regard to migration, especially immigration; to draw the attention of Catholics, especially in the immigration countries, to their duties in the matter of receiving and aiding immigrants; to call the immigrants' attention to their duty of striving to integrate themselves into their new country and to aid them in doing so.

The State and Migration Control

The most fundamental principle which governs all state activity in regard to its population is respect for the rights of individuals and of families. This is far from always recognized in the matter of migration. Legal positivists, for example, hold that the right to migrate is merely the arbitrary consequence of absolute sovereignty. Thus Professor Mayo-Smith writes: "We must disabuse ourselves of the notion that freedom of migration rests on any right of the individual. It is simply a privilege granted by the state, the product of circumstances, the result of experience. The state therefore that conferred the liberty may also withdraw it. . . . The individual has no rights at all in these premises . . . Any privileges he may enjoy rest on diplomatic agreement or on the legislation of the receiving state, not on any virtue residing in him."[4]

Although it based the right to migrate on international agreement rather than natural law, the *Universal Declaration of Human Rights* of the United Nations represents an important step in this area. Article 13 of that declaration states: "1) Everyone has the right to freedom of movement and residence within the borders of each state. 2) Everyone has the right to leave any country, including his own, and to return to his country."

Declaration of principle, however, is one thing; concrete application of it is another. In January, 1963, a joint statement by the International Catholic Migration Commission and other non-governmental organizations presented before the United Nations sub-commission on prevention of discrimination and the protection of minorities, made it clear that there is considerable interference with the right to free migration. Such interference is usually indirect. This statement, dealing with "Discrimination in Respect of the Right of Everyone to Leave any Country, including his own and to Return to his Country," declared that this indirect discrimination usually occurs "as a result of administrative action." It added that "perhaps the most serious form of discrimination occurs when all nationals, with the exception of members of a small governing group, are prevented from going abroad," and argued that "limitations on the right to leave, such as may be required by considerations of national security or national interest, ought not to be imposed except 'within the framework of a general policy permitting everyone to leave the country.' "[5]

Of course freedom to migrate is recognized by most countries; denial of the right is the exception rather than the rule. But some regulation of the exercise of this right is quite common.[6] In the matter of emigration, for example, Syria imposed a total ban in 1959, excepting only those covered by special provisions. More limited restriction has been introduced by India and Ceylon, from which the emigration of only certain categories of workers authorized by the government is permitted, either because it is regarded as economically undesirable or as involving the exploitation of citizens abroad. Freedom to immigrate, on the other hand, is limited by most countries, in the interests of economic and/or cultural protection. The Lebanon, for example, affords residence permits only temporarily and then only to skilled categories of workers. In Western European countries there are no restrictions based on nationality or race, but there is much discrimination in the matter of the status of immigrants.

In 1953 the *Société d'études politiques et sociales* organized a meeting at Louvain to discuss the subject of the state and population questions. From this meeting an important pronouncement was issued, of which the following extract has interest for us here:

The action of the state must be exercised:

a) in respecting the essential prerogatives of persons . . . ; it must confine itself to measures of a collective and indirect character;

b) in the case of excessive demographic pressure, the first duty of the state is to create conditions assuring, for the population as a whole, the necessary means of subsistence; economic development, emigration, etc. . . . ;

c) in the case of encouraging an increase in the birth rate, the economic measures envisaged must not, in themselves, or by the conditions that go with them, constitute direct pressure on married people, but they must tend, without impairing the primordial responsibility of the family, towards the removal of the material obstacles which prevent married couples from having children, maintaining them and educating them.[7]

In other words, the first principle which the state should respect is that people have a right not to have to migrate. In virtue of this, its first duty is to do all in its power to create the economic conditions which will support them at home. Failing this its next duty is to endeavor to see that they are able to emigrate to some other country and settle down there. People have a right to migrate if they need to do so, which right must always be respected. "The natural law itself, no less than devotion to humanity," said Pope Pius XII, "urges that ways of migration be opened to these people."[8]

The Right to Migrate

Pope Pius XII based the right to migrate on three considerations, pertaining respectively to the nature of land, the interest of the individual and the welfare of the family.

The nature of land. In 1948 he wrote specifically on this subject in a letter to the American hierarchy.[9] In this he declared that the natural law itself, no less than devotion to humanity, urges that ways of migrating be opened to those who have to leave their country. The universe was created by God for the good of all men. Hence, wherever land offers the possibility of supporting a large number of people, the sovereignty of the state, although it must be respected, cannot be exaggerated to the point that access to this land is for inadequate or unjustified reasons denied to needy and decent people from other nations, provided, of course, that the public wealth, considered very carefully, does not forbid this.

The interest of the individual. The rights of the individual person and the family are primary. In his Christmas broadcast for 1952, the pope referred specifically to the rights of the individual in the matter of migration.[10] There is, he said, a natural right of the person not to be unduly hindered when emigrating and immigrating—a right which unfortunately is frequently not recognized, or is annulled in practice under the pretext of a common good falsely apprehended or falsely applied, yet sanctioned and made mandatory by legal provisions or administration.

The welfare of the family. Similarly, he connected the right to migrate with the welfare of the family. In June, 1951, in a radio address on the fiftieth anniversary of the encyclical *Rerum Novarum,* he pointed out that the earth, despite its extent of oceans and seas and lakes, mountains and plains, great deserts and trackless lands, is not, at the same time, without habitable regions that are abandoned to wild natural vegetation though well suited to be cultivated by man to satisfy his needs. Recalling the teaching of *Rerum Novarum* concerning the right of the family to an adequate living space, he declared that whenever families found it necessary to seek to migrate to these areas of the world, no obstacle should normally be put in their way.[11]

This is but one of Pius XII's many references to the importance of free migration for the family. In his Christmas message for 1945, he expostulated against the cruelty of the totalitarian state "which sets arbitrary bounds to the necessity and to the right of migration and to the desire to colonize" and called for the introduction of laws made, not in accordance with the whims of passing rulers, but rather according to the pattern of the needs for the world's families. And in his Christmas message for 1948 he recommended that when necessary families be permitted to migrate to more favorable regions rather than have food supplied to them by importation at great expense.

No matter how much a state may wish to see its population grow in numbers, it is not entitled to deny its citizens this right to migrate. By indirect means it may encourage them not to do so, and it may even regulate their use of the right. But it cannot directly deprive them of the right to emigrate. On the contrary, if it is unable to support them itself, it should seek ways and means for them to emigrate to another country if they wish to do so.

The country of immigration should also respect the right to migrate. "Just as your land and fields are great and wide," wrote Pope Pius XII to the Brazilian people in 1952, "so must your hearts be big and open to receive those who want to come and find a new home among you, where they may live honorably with their families." One of the most forceful statements of a country's duty to open its frontiers to immigrants was that of the Australian hierarchy in 1953.[12] It was issued at a time when the state appeared to be deciding that immigration into Australia should be limited with a view to the material prosperity of the country. The bishops underlined the fact that between July, 1947 and September, 1952, Australia's population increased by 1,182,500, of which up to 700,000 were migrants. They admitted that, for a country whose post-war record in the field of politics, economics and industrial relationships had witnessed too many failures, the absorption of up to 700,000 was a positive national achievement, a story of moral and material progress. But they went on to say that by the middle of 1952 this story seemed to have come to an abrupt and disconcerting end. The cause seemed to be the development of unemployment in Australian industry, which revived the fear that migrants would compete for jobs with native born Australians. As a result of these events and pressures, said the bishops, the opinion even of sound members of the population was in a state of thorough confusion, particularly on the moral issue involved in the migration question.

Should the migration program be continued and even accelerated despite the great obstacles and difficulties which it had encountered? This was the great question which the bishops posed. Their own answer was a firm and unwavering "yes." The natural right to immigration and emigration may not normally be denied or modified by the acts of governments. While reasonable regulation of migration is legitimate, to use apparently reasonable regulations as a means of denying the right is not legitimate.

In a land such as Australia whose development has barely begun, how, asked the bishops, could Australians in conscience deny opportunity to those millions, simply to monopolize the continent's resources for themselves? As the spiritual leaders of the Catholic people, the bishops preferred rather to rest their case upon the categorical obligations of the moral law, so clearly put forward by the pope. They were aware of the fact that the criticism would at once be made that in taking such a stand they had no regard for the living standards of the Australian people, and that they ignored the tremendous dangers associated with unemployment, inflation, housing and the rest. Nothing, they protested, could be further from the truth. For they would not admit that, because a particular economic system had ended in failure and that failure involved unemployment and inflation, people should, therefore, reconcile themselves to measures which are morally wrong. And they continued:

> So it is with migration. It is not the lack of resources which have led to the economic impasse into which Australia has fallen. It is the lack of human wisdom, mistakes of national policy which have led us to this stalemate. . . . It is untrue that migration leads necessarily to unemployment. This result follows only when a program of immigration is not complemented by a program of absorption primarily in rural industry. If the program of migration and land settlement are brought into conjunction, par-

ticularly through the technique of colonization, then no unemployment will result. . . . It is untrue that migration is such a
major factor in the development of inflation that it should be dis-
continued. The major cause of inflation lies elsewhere, in the
fact that the Australian economy is geared to too large a degree
to false objectives, to luxury and to unessentials. . . .

Arbitrary Restriction of Migration is Unjust

Despite their vigorous statement that there is a natural right to
migrate, the Australian bishops also declared that "reasonable
regulation of migration is legitimate." Pope Pius XII had admitted that immigration may be limited provided "the common
good, considered very carefully," demands this. But he stressed
that the state must avoid proceeding in such a way that "the
natural right of the person not to be impeded in his emigration
or immigration" is either "not recognized or practically annulled,
on the pretext of a common good falsely interpreted or falsely
applied."

Nevertheless, when this has been said, it is equally true that
he insisted that "in this matter one must be concerned not only
with the interests of the immigrants but also with the good of
the country." He carefully refrained from attacking this or that
nation which had immigration or emigration restrictions in
force,[13] confining himself to outlining the theoretical state of the
question. The central point of his teaching is that there must be
no arbitrary action on the part of the state in introducing migration control. In *Exsul Familia*, for example, he had condemned
"the principles of totalitarianism, of state imperialism and the
irrational nationalism of those who arbitrarily restrict the natural
right of men to migration and pacific colonization on the one
hand, while on the other, they force entire populations to leave
their lands, deporting the inhabitants and barbarously uprooting
citizens from their families, from their homes, from their birth
places," without regard to race or religion. The same teaching
was repeated in 1958 in a letter to the American hierarchy.

In a valuable commentary on *Exsul Familia*, Cardinal Ferretto has summarized as follows the teaching of Pope Pius XII on what the state cannot do by way of migration restriction. The state, he says, cannot "a) arbitrarily restrict the natural right of man to migration and to peaceful colonization; b) deny the right of asylum to those who, for grave reasons, wish to fix their residence elsewhere; c) constrain entire populations to leave their lands; d) impose forced repatriation."[14]

Another commentator has summarized the other side of the pope's teaching: "A state can have valid reasons for restricting and otherwise regulating the inflow of immigrants; but the welfare and security of the immigrant nation is not the only factor to be considered in determining the nature and extent of such regulations. The needs and rights of other people must also be considered, and this is of primary importance when immigration is the only means available for gaining access to the material means for decent human living."[15]

It emerges clearly from all this that the use of the right to migrate can legitimately be regulated in view of the needs of the common good. The important question is what exactly is meant by this? It is hard to see how racial considerations in themselves, for example, could ever constitute sufficient reason for limiting immigration. And, in point of fact, the reasons which are usually given for doing so are mainly economic in character. These are the safeguarding of a high standard of living, the maintenance of a program of full employment and the protecting of the existing level of labor efficiency.

Economists are divided on the question of the effect of immigration on these aspects of a country's economy.[16] One school, which has considerable support in the United States, is of the opinion that unregulated immigration always tends to have adverse economic effects.[17] On the other hand, there are economists who maintain that immigration does not tend, of its very nature, to have unfavorable effects on the economy of the receiving country.[18] We have seen that this attitude has been adopted by the Australian hierarchy. From the historical point of view, there would seem to be much evidence to support it.[19] In the United States there seems to be a constant correlation between immigration cycles and cycles of business prosperity. Again, there seems to be a negative correlation between periods of heavy immigration and periods of employment. Lastly, it is ascertainable that *per capita* incomes have been highest in those states which had the highest percentage of new immigrants in their population. Despite this, however, it is possible to envisage a wave of immigration of such proportions as would severely strain the economy of a country.

The Socio-Economic Effects of Migration

In order to be able to determine fully the factors involved in any particular ethical situation of migration control, one must consider the demographic, economic and social effects of both emigration and immigration on an economy. A few years ago, a comprehensive study of international migration was undertaken with a view to doing just this.[20] Its conclusions were that there is a very great variety between countries in regard to the different effects of emigration and immigration.

The most basic question is whether and how far migratory movements may be said to affect a country's rate of natural population growth. It can be said at once that *emigration* tends to do so by reducing the number of potential couples and therefore the marriage rate. On the other hand, it has also been observed that this reduction is often not proportionate, if the sex distribution of the emigrants is unbalanced. In its turn, *immigration*, while it does tend to increase the rate of natural population growth by increasing the number of possible marriages, due to the special conditions of the receiving country it has frequently been observed that no proportionate increase in the marriage rate results. "Thus it would seem," states the above mentioned

study, "and detailed analysis would probably bear this out, that
the effect of migration on the natural growth of the populations
concerned is not as pronounced as might be thought at first
glance; that the decline of the birth rate in emigration countries,
where compensating factors appear to come into play, is not as
great as might be expected; and that in immigration countries
the rise in the birth rate is likewise held in check by certain
restraining factors."[21]

Of more immediate importance is the effect of migration on
the labor force and, in particular, on its structure and composition. This is something that it is not possible to gauge because
of lack of reliable data up to the present. The most that can be
done is to study it indirectly by way of an examination of the
economic and social effects of migration. By this we mean its
repercussion on real average incomes and on the distribution of
the national income in general. In surveying *emigration* countries
from this point of view, it is necessary to distinguish between the
emigration of unemployed persons on the one hand and of
employed, specially skilled, persons on the other. Emigration of
the former category is usually a good thing; it can even divert
some income from consumption spending to investment. In the
long run, however, its effects can be bad, if economic conditions
improve to such an extent that there is a labor shortage due to
the previous emigration. But it can be said categorically that the
emigration of employed persons is always deleterious; it can
even produce an investment-curtailing effect on an economy.

Turning now to immigration countries, and allowing that, in
general and viewed in the short term, immigration tends to
reduce over-all productivity due to the inflationary pressure
resulting from the employment of people who are not really
needed, the big question is whether, in the long term, immigration will benefit an economy. That it can do so, by stimulating
a declining or too slowly increasing population, or by conducing
to other progress, is certain. But whether and when it will do so

is hard to answer. The most that can be said is that the effects of immigration are likely to be good if the immigrants have generally useful occupations, if their jobs cannot be done by others already in the community, and if their remuneration is equalled by the value of what they produce.

The aforementioned study maintains that the role which immigration has played during the post-war period in the economic development of the United States has been but of secondary and certainly not of essential importance to the country. This will probably continue to be true, according to the study, because of projected improvements in equipment and production methods. The report even states that immigration might actually hinder the rise in productivity and personal income in the United States. On the other hand, it maintains that immigration has been essential to Canada, and that in Australia economic development has been so rapid as to create a strong demand for immigrant labor.[22]

To sum up the debate, it may be accepted that the power of attraction of immigration countries is generally dependent on a labor shortage on the domestic market. Vice-versa, the power of impulsion on the part of emigration countries is generally a surplus of labor on the domestic market. In accordance with whether a country is characterized by a surplus or a shortage of labor, it may be described as suffering from over-population or under-employment from the economic point of view.

Nevertheless—and this is the conclusion of the international survey—the exact relationship between economic development and migration is far from clear. Anomalies occur that defy scientific projection. Sometimes, for example, even when a country is suffering from unemployment, there may in fact be no need for immigration due to the existence in the economy of labor reserves, such as women or farm workers, or the possibility of introducing better mobility into the labor market. Likewise, sometimes even where there is a rapidly increasing population accompanied by emigration, there is in fact no need for this and it could be avoided if better internal mobility were attained. In short, the only conclusion that can be reached with certainty is that there are obvious limitations to any purely theoretical explanation of migration.[23]

The foregoing clarifies the import of Cardinal Ferretto's commentary concerning the difficulty of applying Pope Pius XII's teaching concerning migration: "It is self-evident that the principles enunciated by Pius XII do not apply indiscriminately to every state: they require that the condition of the state be considered, in order to establish whether a country may be classed as one of emigration or of immigration."[24] Of course, migration is not always associated with a need for material goods. Political disturbances, religious convictions, and the desire to colonize are also motives for migration. So too are preference for another government, for a different climate, for a new occupation, for another culture. Again, one may have the desire to do works of charity, or to bring the message of the gospel to other lands. Not all of these motives are as compelling as others, so that one can see why state regulations in the matter could discriminate.

When Can the State Limit Immigration?

State efforts to limit immigration is perhaps the moral aspect of the problem of migration on which the church has had to speak most frequently since the last war. It has been particularly concerned with the morally unjustifiable character of some of the economic reasons which certain countries have been accepting as valid for restricting immigration. That the common good can sometimes demand such restriction has been the Catholic teaching since the time of Vitoria. But it is absolutely essential that any restriction placed on immigration be demanded in each case by the common good properly understood and properly applied. Any restriction that does not comply with these conditions is arbitrary and, therefore, immoral. In other words, the right of restriction "does not come from sovereignty as such, but from the inborn power that every state possesses to work for and protect the common good of its citizens. Hence the power that the State has to pass laws restricting immigration is by its nature limited. Besides, it may not be exercised in order to safeguard particular interests or assume the character of a discriminating measure. The state is not free to act according to its will or whim, but is bound to justify its policy of limitation."[25]

To what extent can purely economic considerations justify such a policy? In this matter Pope Pius XII warned that there is both a true and a false common good. A common good that centers on an economic program rather than a good of the human person is essentially false and misleading.[26] It would seem, therefore, that any restriction of immigration which aimed solely at maintaining a high standard of living is unjustifiable because it subordinates man's personal good to an economic system. Hence when a particular country has a standard of living that is disproportionately high in comparison with that of other overpopulated countries, it may not appeal to the needs of the common good to restrict immigration. The disequilibrium which would ensue from such a policy would be detrimental to the common good of humanity.

Thus G. J. Dullard, commenting on the teachings of Pius XII, has pointed out that, "Certainly economic welfare is an important aspect of the common good, but it is not identical with it. Furthermore, an economy must not be appraised according to the highest degree of quantity, but according to its qualitative elements such as stability and proportionability; and these latter must be considered not merely on the national but on the international plane." He goes on to say that:

It would be false to conclude, however, that economic reasons alone could never be sufficient justification for restricting immigration; but many restrictive laws which are allegedly based on

legitimate economic precautions are not so in fact since they are
the product of false assumptions concerning the effects of immigration or the result of prejudice. Complete exclusion of the
nationals of a foreign state merely because of prejudice against
their nationality and without consideration of personal qualities
would not only violate a fundamental principle of international
law, namely the equality of states, but could also actually deny
the individual's right to migrate. There can be valid reasons for
comparatively severe restriction of immigration by nationals of a
given state, but this is much different from complete exclusion.
Of course, the state always has the right to exclude individual
foreigners who are afflicted with contagious or hereditary diseases;
or those who are vagrants or of immoral character; subversives
and anarchists and others who, because of personal qualities,
would be a real menace to the national welfare, life, honor or
safety.[27]

From this it should be clear that any restriction of immigration
for racial reasons alone is something that cannot be justified. It
is in fact but one example of what we have referred to earlier as
unjust racial discrimination. On the other hand, there is room
for receiving countries to introduce some discrimination relating
to the sociological characteristics of applicants for entry. As also
mentioned before, these can sometimes coincide with racial
characteristics of a cultural order. For this reason the discrimination in question is easily open to being misrepresented as based
on purely racial grounds. Here is a problem that is entirely
unavoidable and to which no easy solution can be proffered. But
while it is important that all migration restriction that is tanta-
mount to unjust racial discrimination should be combated and
eliminated, it is equally important that, where necessary,
legitimate migration control should not fail to be instituted
because of fear of charges of racial bias.

One or two more aspects of the ethics of this question remain
to be outlined. The first of these is that the state is not entitled
to regulate immigration in a way that would discriminate unfairly
between the sexes or between the married and the unmarried.

Archbishop Simonds of Australia found it necessary some years ago to criticize the Australian immigration policy in this respect.

I fear that in working out our great national scheme of migration, the authorities have fallen into the error of considering the migrant as an individual rather than as a person. Our rapidly expanding economy is crying out for more and more working units, and the highest value is placed on single men who will immediately contribute to the needs of industry. Migrant families are regarded as an industrial loss, because many of their young members are of no immediate value on the labor market. Women migrants are not encouraged with the same enthusiasm as are single men. We are thus building up a large group of uprooted workers who have little or no opportunity of developing their personal dignity in family life . . . A policy which denies to tens of thousands of new Australians the normal opportunities of marriage by giving over-all preference to single men, is a thoroughly un-Christian policy, and one that will ultimately yield a harvest of widespread discontent and constitute a serious danger to the moral standards of the community.[28]

The shortage of women among Italian migrants to Australia, for example, has been so great that at one period in Melbourne more than 50 marriages by proxy to girls in Italy were registered each week.[29] This was due to the government's immigration policy which was also criticized sharply by Archbishop Mannix in 1955:

Those in authority are anxious to get more manpower into Australia. . . . Speaking generally they have been bringing young men here from Britain, Italy, Poland, Holland and elsewhere, but they have not been bringing a corresponding number of girls. The migrants coming here are anxious to marry and establish their own homes, but they often have not the opportunity to marry and provide their homes because the young women whom they would wish to marry are left behind in the old countries. I think this aspect of the migration policy deserves looking into, especially for the future. If the young men migrants have not the opportunity of marrying people of their own choice, building their own homes, and having families of their own, the

population of this country in the future is not going to be as
bright as we would wish. I hope therefore the government will
look into the matter.[30]

The Promotion of Organized Emigration

In the field of emigration organization it can safely be said that
Holland is the most advanced country at the present time. For
this reason, the account of the tasks of Catholics in emigration
countries given by the Dutch representative at the Breda
Congress of the International Catholic Migration Commission is
likely to be of particular interest and utility.[31] Herr Kampschoer
said that it is necessary to have two kinds of emigration institutions: institutions whose purpose it is to form a proper public
opinion on emigration, and institutions whose purpose is directly
concerned with the welfare of the immigrants themselves. And
between all these institutions there should exist a close and
continuous co-operation.

Under the first group fall all those activities whereby a
knowledge of Catholic principles regarding emigration may be
spread. The special significance of emigration for the mystical
body of Christ, said Herr Kampschoer, should be stressed.

> History gives a great many proofs of the far-reaching significance
> of the migration of peoples for the world and for the church. . . .
> For us Catholics the Irish emigration in the past is the best proof
> of the influence of emigration in the international Catholic field.
> For present-day Catholic emigrants it should be a privilege to
> help in the expansion of the church which was established in
> many countries by the Irish people or by joining the church in
> those countries where Spanish, Portuguese or Italian emigrants
> brought the Catholic faith.

In this light educational institutions should contribute towards
developing a modern conception of the missions, not in the
traditional sense of the missions to the "heathens," but in the
sense of aid to the already established church. The more specific
emigration institutions will be a success to the extent that this

general educative activity is performed effectively. This activity involves what Herr Kampschoer called "the creation of a disposition, knowledge and professional ability in prospective emigrants of such a nature that a positive integration can take place."

By "disposition" is meant a preparedness to accept without prejudice all the good elements of the new country, an acceptance which must, however, be accompanied by the knowledge that the emigrant himself has something to offer to the immigration country. It is the task of Catholic emigration organizations to warn against negative assimilation and overly pronounced national or racial group formation. The golden mean is a positive integration that will respect the valuable elements of the emigrant's native culture. The "knowledge" and "professional ability" in question mean a grasp of the language of the immigration country and the possession of a skill which will mean an immediate job for the immigrant. These are of particular importance to a country like Holland which has to find emigration outlets for its surplus population. Every emigration country also has duties to the religious instruction of emigrants, the special care that is necessary in the case of female emigrants, and the looking after of the welfare of emigrants' families.

To carry out its activities effectively it is necessary that an emigration organization make its presence felt everywhere in the country, from the local to the national level. Speaking of Catholic emigration organizations, Herr Kampschoer said:

> Committees should be formed locally, which committees should see to it that regular information evenings are held on emigration, on which occasions experts should speak. The members of the committees should also be prepared to give information to prospective emigrants. . . . It shoud also be the task of the local committees to organize preparation courses. The local committees will have their connections with diocesan organizations and with the national emigration organizations.

Once a strong organization for emigrants has been created, it should be possible to secure arrangements with the government whereby financial and other aid would be forthcoming. As already pointed out, the state, as such, has serious obligations towards those of its citizens who have to leave it in order to make a living. It should see that ways of emigration are opened up to them and help them to settle down in the country of their adoption. In the case of some states this aid takes the form of transportation and placement of the emigrants.[32] The provision of hostels is another obvious method. It is an agreed observation that the most dangerous period from the point of view of the morals of the emigrant is that immediately following his arrival in the receiving country. The people whom he meets and the place at which he stays during this period exercise a profound influence, for good or ill, on his character. It is an important part of Catholic migration policy that suitable hostels should be provided at which the emigrants can stay until proper lodgings can be procured for them. Catholic organizations are doing their utmost to provide such hostels.

Some governments also provide such hostels themselves. In 1954 the Spanish government approved plans for the setting up of an emigrants' hostel at the Port of Vigo, at an estimated cost of 6,000,000 pesetas. It includes a lecture hall, dining service for 600 persons, dormitories to accommodate 300 emigrants and many other facilities. Its chief aim is to help to familiarize the emigrants with the new conditions which they have to face in the immigration country.[33]

Similarly, in 1953, a service for the reception and placement of immigrants was opened in Rio de Janeiro. Although officially Catholic, it is aided by a grant from the International Committee for European Migration,[34] which gives financial assistance to about a dozen voluntary migration agencies, including the National Catholic Welfare Conference of the United States and the International Catholic Migration Commission in Geneva.[35]

Immigration Reception and Integration

However, the chief responsibility for the integration of immigrants lies with both church and state in the receiving country. All the emigration country can do is to equip the emigrant with those qualities which will enable him to fit easily into the social and religious life of the new country. True assimilation takes a considerable time, during which the receiving country has important duties towards its immigrants. It is generally agreed that their full integration takes place only in the third generation. It is a process that inevitably takes place eventually, but it can be achieved well or only very imperfectly. Hence the importance of an immigration policy which is conceived with the purpose of achieving full and positive integration by the third generation.[36]

To this end, it must endeavor to provide such conditions as will enable the first generation to overcome the psychological shock of transplantation. This means that the immigrant should not be cut off from the sources of cultural and spiritual nourishment of the old country before he is in a position to avail himself to the full of the riches which his new country has to offer him. In other words, the influence of the old country must provide a backing for immigrants of the first generation, to a lesser extent for those of the second generation, until by the third generation, the descendants of the immigrants can be weaned from it altogether. Clearly this is a policy which slightly retards the rate of assimilation. But forced and sudden integration entails a great psychological shock which can only prove injurious to the immigrant's personality. It can also expose his moral and religious practice to danger. Hence it would be a great error from the point of view of religion to immediately sever the immigrant's links with his mother country.

But error is also possible in the opposite direction. This is to try to maintain permanently, in an artificial way, the links which

connect the immigrants' descendants with the old country. The
result of this would only be to keep them strangers and to cause
their faith to be regarded as an alien creed. It is good for neither
church nor state for Catholic emigration countries to seek to
create national colonies in sovereign lands.[37] But it is clear too
that the avoidance of this depends also in large measure on the
reception that is accorded to the migrants by the immigration
country.

At the Breda Congress of 1954 an account of the activities of
Catholic organizations in this area was given by Monsignor
George Crennan, director of the Federal Catholic Immigration
Committee of Australia.[38] Their field of activity, he said, reaches
down from the hierarchy itself, in the countries of immigration,
to priests and religious and, in a particular way, to those clergy
whose special task is the spiritual care of immigrants. It extends,
too, to governmental and non-governmental bodies. It involves
the thought and planning of organizations, social, political and
economic. In a rather special way it makes demands upon the
individual Catholic who in personal intercourse with the immigrants is in a position to render services most effective for the
realization of a harmonious and happy integration of the immigrant into parochial and community life. In this respect older
immigrants, somewhat integrated already, can do much in giving
confidence to the newcomer.

Monsignor Crennan went on to say that the parochial clergy
are called upon to exercise unfailing charity and zeal towards the
immigrant who, not infrequently, has suffered distress, even
grave injustice and persecution, and who may easily find himself
a stranger even in the church which he enters to pray. The
provision of national priests or missionaries for immigrants was
an important directive of the apostolic constitution *Exsul Familia*,
and its implementation is vital for the proper spiritual care of
immigrants. The work of these priests, though of temporary
duration, serves to procure a happy transition from the language,

devotions and practices of the old land to those of the new. But combined with their work must be the work of the parochial clergy, to the end that there shall be a gradual fusion of old and new parishioners to form one united parochial family. Such organized spiritual care must extend also to immigrants who have settled in sparsely populated areas. Here there is work for itinerant chaplains.

As far as the state is concerned, it has the duty to see that there is no discrimination against immigrants in the matter of assigning jobs or finding them a place in the economy. In 1955 Archbishop Mannix strongly criticized the Australian government's policy of giving little encouragement to immigrants to settle in the rural areas:

> The migration policy of the government has not been as wisely directed as it might have been. When the government embarked upon a policy of bringing people here from overseas, one would have imagined that an endeavor would have been made as far as possible to settle migrants in the country instead of huddling the vast majority of them in the big cities. . . . An Act of Parliament was passed to facilitate the settlement of migrants on the land in Victoria, but I understand that within the last few days this Act has been repealed. Why this should be done I don't know. It certainly is a reversion to the policy which, from the very beginning, was faulty.[39]

Indeed it is safe to say that if such a policy were a deliberate attempt to force immigrants into industry it would not only be unwise and faulty but unjust. This matter is an extremely important one at the present day, for many of the emigrant families from Europe are agricultural. Since World War II, some 300,000 exclusively agricultural families have taken refuge from the Soviet Zone in Western Germany. Only about 50,000 of them have been able to resettle on the land. Although the possibilities of an intra-European migration of this class have been investigated,[40] it would seem that the emigration of agricultural workers from Western Europe will continue for many years to come.

Social justice demands that under-populated farming countries should place no difficulties in the way of these immigrants' settling on the land.[41]

Experienced workers are all agreed that any work for migrants will be quite defective without international contacts between the organizations concerned. The International Catholic Migration Commission is already an instrument to bring about such contacts. The following resolutions, issued from its 1954 Congress, were addressed to National Catholic Migration Organizations all over the world. These were urged: a) to exert every effort to inform the public and influence legislation in migration and population matters; b) to draw the attention of the public, and especially of the press and the clergy, to refugee problems; c) to establish in every country, besides the National Catholic Emigration Committee, diocesan or local committees for emigration; d) to establish information centers for immigrants in each diocese or city where the need is felt; e) to publish two-language booklets (in the language of the receiving and departure countries) with the names of Catholic organizations, addresses of priests, etc.; f) to explore the possibility of establishing agricultural families on land (and realizing certain pilot projects as extensively as possible); g) to contribute to the International Catholic Migration Commission; h) to cooperate more closely with the International Catholic Commission's Information Center.[42]

The Teaching of "Pacem In Terris"

Three directives concerning migration are contained in *Pacem in Terris*.[43] The encyclical states: "Every man should be allowed to retain or, if he should so desire, to change his place of residence within his own country, or, if there be good cause for doing so, to take up his abode in another." The first directive, then, is that, within his own country, every citizen (who is not justly detained by the state for good reasons) has a right to freedom of movement and settlement. Secondly, everyone has a right to leave his country if he has just reasons for doing so, and, thirdly, he has a corresponding right to enter and reside in other countries. These directives are intended to censure both the unfair barriers to immigration that are sometimes erected by countries that could afford a greater intake, and those states which unjustly prevent their citizens from leaving them if they wish to do so.

We should be attentive to the wording of the declaration. Pope John was concerned with the right of migration in general. The Vatican Press English version speaks of the right to "emigrate," the Italian version of the right to "immigrate"; it is better to speak more broadly of the right to "migrate." The French text is more faithful to the Latin original (*Alias civitates petere in iisque domicilium suum collocare*). Every man, it says, has a right to go abroad and to settle there (*de se rendre à l'étranger et de s'y fixer*). The significance of this statement about migration in *Pacem in Terris* is not that the encyclical is thereby breaking new ground in Catholic teaching, but the fact that in international documents the world community has until now accepted only the right to emigrate.

The encyclical defends the right to free migration "if there be a good cause" for migrating, but presumably not necessarily otherwise. In other words, the exercise of the right to migrate can be restricted and there seems to be no sufficient reason for confining the ethical possibility of such restriction exclusively to immigration.

Apart altogether from the question of migration control, both emigration and immigration countries have duties to the welfare of their migrants. This is a matter that is of immense importance where there is question of racial migration. It is a work that is best performed by voluntary bodies. In general it relates to the promotion of the integration of migrants, and it is governed by the same fundamental principles no matter what kind of migration integration is in question.

Notes

1. Cardinal Ferretto, in G. Tessarolo (*ed.*), *The Church's Magna Charta for Migrants* (New York, 1962), p. 154.

2. "Attitude Chrétienne en face des Migrations," report to the Breda Congress, 1954.

3. Cf. Mgr. Swanstrom, "The Christian Attitude towards Migration," Breda Congress, 1954.

4. *Emigration and Immigration* (London, 1960).

5. Cf. "Right of Everyone to Leave Any Country," *Migration News*, 1963, No. 2. Cf. also Rev. Albert Verdoodt, "Fifteenth Anniversary of the Universal Declaration of Human Rights," in *Migration News*, 1963, No. 6.

6. Cf. *International Migration, 1945–57* (International Labor Office, Geneva, 1959), p. 212 seq.

7. Cf. P. de Pie, "The State and the Birth Rate," in *The I.C.M.C. News*.

8. Letter to Archbishop McNicholas, December 24, 1948.

9. Cited in G. Tessarolo, *The Church's Magna Charta for Migrants* (New York, 1962).

10. Cf. Tessarolo, *op. cit.;* also J. Newman, "Social Documents: The Catholic Attitude to Migration," in *Christus Rex*, IX (1955) No. 1.

11. Cf. *ibid.*

12. Cf. *ibid.*

13. Cf. A. Zimmerman, *Overpopulation: A Study of Papal Teachings on the Problem* (Washington, 1957).

14. In Tessarolo, *op. cit.*

15. G. J. Dullard, "The Right to Immigrate and the Teaching of Pope Pius XII," in *Migration News* (1959), No. 6.

16. Cf. A. Perotti, "Economic Motives Limiting the Right of Immigration: Their Moral Justification," paper to Breda Congress, 1954.

17. E.g., A. H. Hansen, *Full Recovery or Stagnation* (New York, 1949); J. Isaac, *Economics of Migration* (London, 1947).

18. E.g., M. Melnyk, *Les ouvrières étrangeres en Belgique* (Louvain, 1951).

19. Cf. Perotti, *op. cit.*

20. *International Migration, 1945–57* (Geneva, 1959).

21. *Ibid.*, pp. 332–333.

22. *Ibid.*, p. 332 seq.

23. *Ibid.*, p. 232.

24. In Tessarolo, *op. cit.*, pp. 161–162.

25. Cf. A. Perotti, *op. cit.*

26. Cf. Christmas Message, 1952.

27. *Op. cit.*, p. 6.

28. Cf. *The Advocate* (Melbourne), July 21, 1955.

29. Cf. "Spotlight on Australia," in *The Irish Independent*, March 6, 1956.

30. *The Advocate*, March 17, 1955. Cf. also *ibid.*, March 31, 1955, and July 7, 1955. On the right of the state to limit emigration in certain circumstances, see J. Newman, "Emigration and the Faith," in *Christus Rex*, X (1956), No. 4, and *Principles of Peace* (Oxford, 1964), pp. 89–93. The question has been discussed in the context of Irish emigration to Britain by Dr. Alfred O'Rahilly in "Ban these Emigrants," *The Catholic Standard*, June 12, 1944. Cf. also *The Irish Independent*, December 23, 1963 and February 25, 1965. As the matter does not concern racial migration problems, we omit treatment of it here.

31. Cf. G. W. Kampschoer, "The Task of Catholics in Emigration, Countries," paper read at Breda Congress, 1954.

32. Cf. J. B. Lanctot, "The Transportation, Reception, Placement Adaptation, Settlement and Integration of Migrants," report to Breda Congress, 1954.

33. Cf. *The I.C.M.C. News*, April, 1954.

34. Cf. *ibid.*, October, 1953.

35. Cf. "ICEM-Supported Activities of the Voluntary Agencies," in *The I.C.M.C. News*, June, 1954.

36. Cf. G. Rochcau, "Emigration and Assimilation," in *The I.C.M.C. News*, February, 1954.

37. Cf. *ibid.*

38. Cf. "Tasks of Catholics in Immigration Countries," Breda Congress, 1954.

39. Cf. *The Advocate* (Melbourne), October 27, 1955.

40. Cf. E. Rochefort, "A Catholic Attitude before the Problem of intra-European Migration," Breda Congress, 1954.

41. Cf. W. Boyens, "General Principles of Agricultural Migration," in *The I.C.M.C. News*.

42. Cf. "Summary of the Resolutions of the International Catholic Migration Congress, 1954," in *The I.C.M.C. News*, October, 1954.

43. Cf. J. Newman, *Principles of Peace* (Oxford, 1964), pp. 89–93.

For Further Reading

S. Coderre, *La doctrine de l'église sur les migrations d'après les documents officielles et magistère*, Montreal, 1955.

Margaret Feeny, *Catholics and World Poverty*, London, 1960.

G. Ferretto, *La Chiesa e le Migrazioni*, Rome, 1960.

L'Integrazione degli immigrati Cattolici secondo la costituzione apostolica "Exsul Familia," Rome, 1960.

Mgr. G. Kelly, *Overpopulation: A Catholic View*, New York, 1960.

J. J. Mol, *Churches and Immigrants*, The Hague, 1961.

Rev. A. Zimmerman, *Catholic Viewpoint on Overpopulation*, New York, 1961.

Pius XII and International Migration, Washington, 1959.

Nihil Obstat: Carroll E. Satterfield
Censor Librorum

Imprimatur: ✠ Lawrence Cardinal Shehan, D.D.
Archbishop of Baltimore
February 15, 1967